# Counseling Survivors of Religious Abuse

This book identifies and analyzes the forms, causes, and potential treatments of religious abuse. Religious abuse can include experiences of sexual, physical, emotional, spiritual, and mental abuse connected to a religious context. The book will help readers understand different types of religious abuse, including where the perpetrator is a religious leader, a group, or a system, as well as when there is an overtly spiritual element connected to the justification for the abuse. It also describes common experiences of those who have experienced religious abuse and some treatment approaches that will be useful to mental health providers when their clients present with these experiences. The rigorous scholarly approach of this book provides an academically grounded insight into this complex topic. As such, it will be a key reference for those studying and working in Religious Studies, Religion and Psychology, the Sociology of Religion, and Counseling and Mental Health.

**Paula J. Swindle** is Associate Professor of Counseling at Lenoir-Rhyne University in Hickory, NC, and has over 24 years of experience as a clinical mental health counselor and supervisor. She owns the Center for Healing Religious Harm, PLLC, which provides counseling and consultation services, and co-hosts the podcast "Sacred Intersections" which examines the intersection of mental health, religion, and religious abuse.

**Craig S. Cashwell** is Professor in the Department of School Psychology and Counselor Education at William & Mary and an American Counseling Association (ACA) Fellow. Additionally, Craig maintains a part-time private practice focusing on couple counseling, addictions counseling, and spiritual and religious issues. He has over 150 publications, including five books, and has received multiple research awards.

**Jodi L. Tangen** is Associate Professor and Program Coordinator at North Dakota State University. Her research interests center on counselor education, spirituality, and teacher and counselor development. She is passionate about training counselors and enjoys teaching courses such as Counseling Techniques and Counseling across the Lifespan. In her free time, she hangs out with her energetic little kids.

# Routledge Focus on Religion

**Trump and History**
Protestant Reactions to 'Make America Great Again'
*Matthew Rowley*

**Theology and Climate Change**
*Paul Tyson*

**Religion and Euroscepticism in Brexit Britain**
*Ekaterina Kolpinskaya and Stuart Fox*

**Owning the Secular**
Religious Symbols, Culture Wars, Western Fragility
*Matt Sheedy*

**Cross-Cultural and Religious Critiques of Informed Consent**
*Edited by Joseph Tham, Alberto García Gómez, and Mirko Daniel Garasic*

**Worldview Religious Studies**
*Douglas J Davies*

**White Evangelicals and Right-Wing Populism: How Did We Get Here?**
*Marcia Pally*

**Rape Culture in the House of David: A Company of Men**
*Barbara Thiede*

**Counseling Survivors of Religious Abuse**
*Paula J. Swindle, Craig S. Cashwell, and Jodi L. Tangen*

For more information about this series, please visit: www.routledge.com/Routledge-Focus-on-Religion/book-series/RFR

# Counseling Survivors of Religious Abuse

Paula J. Swindle, Craig S. Cashwell, and Jodi L. Tangen

Routledge
Taylor & Francis Group

LONDON AND NEW YORK

First published 2024
by Routledge
4 Park Square, Milton Park, Abingdon, Oxon OX14 4RN

and by Routledge
605 Third Avenue, New York, NY 10158

*Routledge is an imprint of the Taylor & Francis Group, an informa business*

© 2024 Paula J. Swindle, Craig S. Cashwell, and Jodi L. Tangen

The right of Paula J. Swindle, Craig S. Cashwell, and Jodi L. Tangen to be identified as authors of this work has been asserted in accordance with sections 77 and 78 of the Copyright, Designs and Patents Act 1988.

All rights reserved. No part of this book may be reprinted or reproduced or utilised in any form or by any electronic, mechanical, or other means, now known or hereafter invented, including photocopying and recording, or in any information storage or retrieval system, without permission in writing from the publishers.

*Trademark notice*: Product or corporate names may be trademarks or registered trademarks, and are used only for identification and explanation without intent to infringe.

*British Library Cataloguing-in-Publication Data*
A catalogue record for this book is available from the British Library

ISBN: 9780367465445 (hbk)
ISBN: 9781032549422 (pbk)
ISBN: 9781003029465 (ebk)

DOI: 10.4324/9781003029465

Typeset in Times New Roman
by codeMantra

# Contents

**SECTION I**
**Overview** 1

1 Integrating Spirituality in Counseling 3
2 Defining Religious Abuse 25
3 Common Experiences of Victims of Religious Abuse 32
4 Assessing Religious Abuse 38
5 Characteristics of Healthy and Harmful Religious Systems 41
6 Common Victim Populations 44

**SECTION II**
**Ethics** 49

7 Ethical Principles in the Treatment of Religious Abuse 51
8 Application of Ethics in Treating Religious Abuse 64

**SECTION III**
**Treatment Approaches** 75

9 The Importance of a Trauma-Informed Approach 77
10 The Healing Process 79

vi  *Contents*

11  Interventions for Religious Abuse             81
12  Supervision and Consultation                  84
13  Summary                                       86

   *Index*                                        89

# Section I
# Overview

# 1 Integrating Spirituality in Counseling

As a starting place for this book, we believe that there is much that is good about religion.

Religious communities of all faiths provide knowledge that helps people to understand and make meaning of their lives, participate in meaningful rituals, find forgiveness for misdeeds, comfort during hard times, and a social community of like-minded believers. At its best, religion provides a structure within which people can experience transformation and connection, and grow spiritually. As authors, each of us has a long history of participating in organized religion. We consider ourselves to be spiritual seekers who have found great wisdom, support, and comfort from our respective experiences within organized religion. At its best, religion is invaluable, perhaps even essential, to many people.

Religion at its best is good. But what about when the people within religious communities are not at their best? What about the shadow side of religion? What about when there is a twisting of the sacred in a way that does great damage to an individual or a group of individuals? While we consider ourselves people of faith, we are also mental health professionals with a combined 60+ years of clinical experience. Over the years, we have heard stories and witnessed countless cases where the support of a loving and nurturing religious community and religious leaders was a critical part of the client's healing work. Unfortunately, however, over these same years, we have sat with hundreds of clients who came to us having experienced abuse within their religious community. In many cases, they came seeking support specifically for the religious abuse. Interestingly, however, in other cases they presented with common presenting issues (anxiety, depression, addictions) and were not consciously aware of the religious abuse they had experienced and, in many cases, how this connected to their psychological struggles. Not all people who experience religious abuse experience traumatic symptoms as a result, but many do. Throughout the course of this book, we will explore various forms of religious abuse. Within a trauma-informed lens, we want to change the question for clients from "What is wrong with me?" to "What happened to me?" It is our intent, however, as mental health professionals to go beyond the "what happened" narrative, as important as that narrative is, to look also at the impact of religious abuse on individuals and groups marginalized by the abuse. Further, we also want to provide some preliminary information on what the path of healing from religious abuse might look like.

As a starting point to this conversation, we will explore psychospiritual integration or the integration of a client's religion into the counseling process. Our primary frame of reference and experience is working in a secular counseling setting so those who counsel from an overtly religious perspective or in a religious setting may need to adapt some of the narrative throughout this book. What we are exploring here is the work of mental health professionals who recognize the value of carefully assessing religious and spiritual beliefs, practices, and experiences in the therapy process. While this will not be germane for some clients, many come to us with a history (be it primarily positive, negative, or mixed) with organized religion that informs their worldview and, in many cases, is inextricably interwoven with their worldview, core beliefs, and mental health (or lack thereof). Because some mental health professionals are hesitant to integrate the client's religious belief systems into the therapy process, before we turn our attention more fully to religious abuse, we explore the process of psychospiritual integration.

## Religion and Spirituality in the Therapy Process

Historically, therapists have been trained to assess and understand the various identities of an individual, often presenting cases to consultants and peers by starting with some of these identities. Imagine, for example, a case staffing where a therapist begins presenting a case to a group:

> The client is a 47-year-old African American male who is married and he and his wife have 3 children, ages 14, 11, and 8. He grew up in poverty but now owns his own company that is thriving and he and his family are upper middle class. He reports being active in his African Methodist Episcopal (AME) Zion religious community, which he describes as the denomination in which he grew up and, in fact, he attends the same church in which he grew up. He presents with anxiety stemming from recent conversations with his pastor after congregants in the church told the pastor that the client's oldest son is saying he thinks he might be transgender and the pastor told the client that "being transgendered" (sic) is an abomination against God and that his son either needs to get right with God or he will be asked not to attend this church.

While there are fascinating conversations to be had about cases such as these, many of those will be left to subsequent chapters in this book. For now, however, consider only the complexity of identities presented in this brief introduction to the case and, more importantly, the potential *intersectionality* of these identities. Clearly, there are a number of identities that are listed in this simple case introduction. Based on the therapist's report, the client appears to be

- Middle-aged
- African-American
- Male and presumably cisgender
- A husband
- A father
- Grown up in poverty (which may have psychological implications)
- Affluent
- A business owner
- Religious and long-term attendance and service within his church; the therapist's report highlights the salience of this identity.

Each of these identities defines this client to some extent and in certain contexts. We do not yet know many things about this client, however, most notably how these identities intersect. How, for example, does this client make meaning of moving from poverty to affluence? How does he balance his family identity, work identity, and religious identity? How do his various identities inform how he personally thinks and feels about his child questioning their gender identity? How do his various identities inform how he is hearing these words from his pastor and subsequent actions that he might take? What is critical in therapy, then, is understanding the *salience* of these identities, supporting the client in making this more explicit, and understanding how they intersect to inform this client's life experience, including this current crisis which appears to be occasioning anxiety.

Based on this initial case presentation, though, we might assume that this client's religious identity is highly salient, which is not uncommon (Cashwell & Young, 2020). Researchers have examined the salience of religious and spiritual identities and found that approximately 93% of the U.S. population reports some type of religious or spiritual identity with approximately 75% of people having a religious identity (Pew Research Center, 2015). As we will explore throughout this book, when religious abuse occurs, the resulting trauma often is devastating, and when the religious or spiritual identity is highly salient, the impact may be even more damaging.

Before turning our attention to the impact of betrayal trauma occasioned by religious abuse in subsequent chapters, however, we focus first on how therapists might think about the process of integrating spirituality and religion into the therapy process. This offers context for the work when a client presents with religious abuse.

## Defining Religion and Spirituality

In navigating this book, it may be useful to know how we think of *religion* and *spirituality*. To some extent, *religion* is the easier of the two to define.

Organized religion provides a social context in which beliefs, practices, and experiences occur. To that end, religion is institutional, creedal, and typically socially defined (Young & Cashwell, 2020). The three largest religions, by affiliation, in the United States are the three primary Western religions, namely Christianity (70.6%), Judaism (1.9%), and Islam (.9%), followed by two Eastern religions, namely Buddhism and Hinduism, each of which constitutes about 7% of the U.S. population (Pew Center, 2015).

Spirituality, on the other hand, is a more complex and fluid construct, making it more challenging to provide a universal definition. For individuals, spiritual expression is vast and difficult to capture in words. For some, it is primarily about a belief system. For others, it is more about practices and experiences. For all, it is, to some extent, a developmental phenomenon as it evolves over time. This developmental, contextual, and individual framework requires a definition that is broad and inclusive. To that end, we use a definition developed by Young and Cashwell (2020) that spirituality is "the universal human capacity to experience self-transcendence and sacred immanence, with resulting increases in self-other compassion and love" (p. 12).

In the next section, we will discuss the importance of assessing the unique relationship between religion and spirituality at an individual level, that is, how the two "dance" together for an individual client, including the possibility that an individual's spirituality is experienced outside of the context of organized religion, which seems to account for about 20% of people in the United States (Harris, 2014). For now, though, we want to unpack this definition further in the context of those who experience their spirituality primarily within the context of organized religion, which constitutes a substantial percentage of U.S. citizens, with consideration of the application of the definition to issues of religious abuse.

We believe this definition of spirituality is short and concise, but rich with facets critical to an understanding of religious abuse. We discuss these briefly here:

- *Universal* – Spirituality is available and accessible to all, not simply a chosen few. A classic example of this is from the Christian tradition where Matthew 22:14 is commonly translated as *Many are called (or invited), but few are chosen*. Translated in this manner, pastors often misuse this scripture to establish a religious community that looks more like a country club than a spiritual community, where there are clear in-groups and out-groups, and many are *othered* and marginalized. Some biblical scholars, however, suggest that this is poor translation of the original text and that a better translation would be something like *I am calling all of you, but so few of you allow yourselves to be chosen*. This translation reads quite differently, suggesting that all are welcomed if they will only receive the call or invitation. When religion *others* people who are often also marginalized by society, when the very community that should be a safe haven for all

chooses who gets in the club and who does not, the result can often be abuse and a traumatic experience for the individual.
- *Capacity* suggests that all people have the potential to cultivate and experience spirituality as part of their life journey. It also suggests that not all will potentiate their capacity. One framework for a person's capacity to develop spiritually is captured in the eightfold path of Buddhism which encourages right view, right resolve, right speech, right conduct, right livelihood, right effort, right mindfulness, and right samadhi. Samadhi refers to unity with the highest reality, which for those with a theistic religion can easily be translated into right unity with their Higher Power. Capacity, then, is cultivated through spiritual practice, beliefs, and actions. Religious abuse can occur when a charismatic leader pushes practices, beliefs, and behaviors on followers with no allowance for disagreement or debate, which is the point at which doctrine becomes dogma. Anyone who questions the dogma is *othered* and, in some cases, ostracized from the community.
- *Experience* suggests that spirituality is not solely about a belief system but rather includes spiritual practices and behaviors that result in spiritual growth and change. An example would be a person who practices a form of contemplative practice consistent with their belief systems that supports their development of more nondual thinking. In some cases, however, the religious community may be operating at a dualistic level. Imagine, for example, the tension for a client who reports practicing contemplative prayer for many years and is struggling in her long-term religious community that marginalizes women and members of the LGBTQ+ (Lesbian, Gay, Bisexual, Transgender, Queer plus) community.
- *Self-transcendence* suggests that spiritual development is a true path only if it ultimately decenters the self in the conversation. The first part of the life journey is about building a sense of self, often a sense of self that is separate and disconnected from others. Ultimately, though, this sense of separateness fades and there is recognition that everything belongs, all is connected, and our lives are best lived in service to others. That is, transcending the personal ego is part of the spiritual journey. Here, religious abuse can occur when beliefs are imposed that diminish the individual in a shame-based way. One cannot transcend an ego that has been traumatized and bound in shame. Rather, we tend to recapitulate this trauma in various ways, working unconsciously to make true this lie we have been told and cannot begin the work of self-transcendence. Instead, we can get caught in a trap of chasing acceptance (from both self and others) and always trying to be "good enough" to earn favor (from either God or other people), a process that is prepersonal (ego-building) rather than transpersonal (beyond the ego) (Wilber, 2000). Interestingly, behaviors, such as tirelessly serving others, can look similar for people at both the prepersonal and transpersonal levels, but differ significantly in intent (e.g., building up self vs. genuinely serving others).

- *Sacred immanence* recognizes that spirituality dwells within each of us. Whether the individual holds a belief of a Higher Power or believes, as the Buddha stated, that we all have innate Buddha nature or enlightenment within us, spirituality cultivates receptivity to this Presence. We resonate with the word "Mindbodyspirit," which recognizes that the mind, the body, and spirit are all interconnected and sacred. For those with a belief in God, there is an indwelling of this Spirit within each of us in the present moment. As such, our bodies are a temple for this Spirit which can only be experienced in the present moment. Religious abuse can occur, for example, when teachings create body, thought, or sexual shame or treat the present moment as only a moment to be "used" to get to an afterlife, psychologically cultivating shame and a sense that nothing in the "now" is good, but rather just a path to an afterlife.
- *Increases in self-other compassion and love* suggests the most important measure of whether the spiritual path is true or not. Whatever one believes to be true, whatever spiritual practices one undertakes, all is for naught if we do not grow in our capacity to love and hold compassionate space, for both ourselves and others.

Before turning our attention to the various ways in which people connect or disconnect their religion and spirituality, we want to make one more point. In the Christian tradition, there is sacred text that suggests the individual should *Be perfect, therefore, as your heavenly Father is perfect* (Matthew 5:48, NIV). The pursuit of perfection, however, is one of the greatest sources of shame and mental illness known to modern society. How can this be reconciled? Some theologians would argue that this is an aspirational ideal, which certainly makes sense at an objective level. Unfortunately, however, our experiences over the years with clients who are religious lead us to conclude that while some might hold this aspirational stance, far more often the result of perfectionism is pervasive shame and inadequacy, with subsequent mental health struggles including depression, anxiety, and addictions.

Alternatively, some biblical scholars (Klotz, 2001) suggest that the Greek word translated as *perfect* is better translated as *complete* or *whole*. Accordingly, one stance we take throughout this book is that what is true spiritually is healthy psychologically. If some belief or practice makes one less psychologically well or cultivates struggles with mental illness (e.g., anxiety or depression), then it is not a capital-T Truth. Our goal is not to be perfect but to be more whole, more complete. It is no coincidence that the words *whole, healing,* and *holy* all derive from the same root. An example of where this turns abusive occurs when religious teachers promote self-loathing and self-hatred, ostensibly to encourage reliance on a Higher Power. Unfortunately, however, we have seen in our respective counseling practices *many* people for whom the single greatest barrier in their spiritual journey was a sense of not deserving, not being worthy, or not being good enough to be known and loved by

God. Religious or spiritually oriented teachings, practices, and actions that cultivate less psychological health for an individual are, by extension, abusive and potentially traumatic.

## The Dance between Religion and Spirituality

If approximately 75% of the population identifies with some organized religion (Pew Center, 2015) and approximately another 20% (Harris, 2014) identify as spiritual but not religious, then a substantial percentage of clients will walk in to the therapy session with a religious and/or spiritual worldview. Whether this identity involves connection with a religious or spiritual community, denomination or sect, engagement with beliefs or practices (mainstream or otherwise), the religious/spiritual worldview of these clients cannot be ignored in the therapy room. To do so minimizes the impact of the therapy process, at best, and, at worst, does harm to the client (Cashwell & Pulgar, 2019). For some people, a religious or spiritual identity will be salient and, for some, the *most* salient part of their identity, that is, the part of the self with which they most relate, identifying themselves first and sometimes entirely by their religious or spiritual worldview. Further, it seems clear from hundreds of studies that religion and spirituality can have a positive impact on psychological and physical health (Koenig, King, & Carson, 2012). Therapists, then, must be equipped to address religious and spiritual issues with clients (Cashwell & Young, 2020).

The relationship between the religious and spiritual life is idiosyncratic. In cases where the religious identity is salient to the client, then, therapists must take the time to fully unpack the nuances of the religious and spiritual life for the individual. Although, as noted earlier in this chapter, many distinguish between religion and spirituality and, indeed, some define themselves as one but not the other, it is important to understand that for many people their religious and spiritual lives are inextricably interwoven, to the extent that conversations that attempt to separate the two may, at least initially, be confusing to the client. In contrast, a rapidly growing group in the United States is those who identify as spiritual but not religious, eschewing organized religion but following some thread of beliefs, practices, and experiences that constitute a personal spirituality. A third group practices organized religion more out of habit and/or fear than a quest for spiritual growth. Such people rarely engage in disciplined spiritual practices, have limited spiritual experiences, and might best be understood as religious but not spiritual. Finally, it seems important to mention that clients will come to us either from a place where neither religion nor spirituality is a salient aspect of their identity *or* from a place where they do not wish to discuss their religion or spirituality in therapy. Client autonomy should be honored.

The primary focus of this book is *religious abuse*, that is, abuse that causes the abused individual (or family system, in many cases) to experience trauma, which will be defined and described throughout this book. While we are primarily focusing on abuse that happens within the context of organized religion, it is important to highlight that not all spiritually oriented abuse happens within organized religions. There are many examples of gurus and spiritual teachers who would not describe their work as religious *per se* who abuse those who follow them. Often borne of spiritual narcissism and entitlement, these charismatic leaders do great psychological, emotional, and spiritual harm to those who blindly follow them. Taken to a sufficiently extreme level, this becomes, by definition, a cult.

Within the context of organized religion, there can be much that is so sacred and so beautiful. Rituals, practices, community, support, friendships, teaching and learning, and serving others, both those within the religious community and those in the surrounding area are all examples of sacred aspects of religion. Religious communities can be communities of support that nurture healthy spiritual and psychological development among its members. It is considered sacred space, in and of itself, by many adherents. What happens, though, when the sacred is twisted. Make no mistake, the types of abuse that we will chronicle in this book, grounded in our own experiences as therapists and members of religious communities ourselves, along with what is written in the scholarly literature, are all examples of a twisting of the sacred in a way that is damaging to individuals, couples, and families. Unfortunately, it occurs with children and adults of all ages. The impact can be immense, even when it is unconscious, and the consequences can be far-reaching and long-term.

Whatever the presenting issue, people come to therapy in search of healing, wholeness, and a sense of purpose, rather new or renewed. This book explores what it is like to sit in the "other chair" and hear these stories, hold space for the pain, and provide support for healing and, in many instances, even growth out of the pain that these people are experiencing. While many clients explicitly bring narratives of religious abuse into an initial session, others relate what has happened to them without realizing that it was abusive or that they are experiencing trauma symptoms.

## Ethics of Psychospiritual Integration

The issue of integrating religion and spirituality in the counseling process is not without controversy. These are long-standing controversies dating back to Freud who considered organized religion a disavowal of reality and a regression to infantile narcissism. This is to be contrasted against the early works of a contemporary of Freud's, William James, who considered what we might now call spiritual or transpersonal experiences to be highly salient in the therapeutic and healing process (James, 2012). Similarly, another contemporary of Freud, Carl Jung, split with Freud's school of thoughts, in part, because he found the search for meaning a deeply spiritual process (Jung,

1960). There remain clinicians and scholars in the mental health field who believe that matters of religion and spirituality should solely be referred out to clergy. While we agree that some issues should be deferred and referred back to the client's clergy, in many cases this runs the risk of further fragmenting the client, whereas competent and ethical integration of religion and spirituality in the therapy process enhances the likelihood of wholeness and optimal functioning. Such referrals also assume that the clergy will interact with the parishioner in a way that fosters spiritual growth and psychological wellness. As we will see from numerous case examples throughout this book, this is not always the case.

For clients with a salient religious or spiritual identity, whether they are presenting with religious abuse or not, failing to integrate their religion and spirituality in some way, even if simply giving space in the therapy rooms for client exploration around religious and spiritual matters, is to deny a critical aspect of their culture and developmental history. Can you imagine ignoring information related to a client's gender identity, racial identity, or disability status. Yet, just like each of these areas, religion and spirituality are considered a federally protected class, meaning that it is illegal to discriminate based on this. We would go so far as to suggest that ignoring the client's religious and/or spiritual life is unethical because it is discriminatory.

Unfortunately, however, many therapists fear talking about religion or spirituality in the therapy room out of a fear of somehow imposing values, an ethical breach that will be discussed further in Chapters 7 and 8. In our experience as clinical supervisors, we have watched students and professionals err on all sides of this dilemma. That is, we have seen clinicians ignore religious and spiritual information and impose personal values on the client, and we have also seen mental health workers respond to client statements in a way that demeaned the client's religious and spiritual beliefs, practices, or experiences. This triad of ignoring, imposing, or demeaning client spirituality has substantially negative impact on clients, often impacting not only their immediate experience in therapy but also their later decisions to attend therapy (Cashwell & Pulgar, 2019). At the same time, we have observed the power of psychospiritual integration, conducted with compassion and cultural humility by the therapist, profoundly enhance the healing work of the client.

Concerns about imposing values and, even if inadvertently, demeaning the client's religion and spirituality are not to be taken lightly. How, then, do clinicians hold the sacred space that these conversations deserve? The single most important consideration is cultural humility in which the client is centered first and foremost in the conversation. As a clinician, *always* recognizing that you are not the expert on the client's religious and spiritual life and, particularly in instances where religion and spirituality are salient aspects of the client's identity, understanding the sacred nature of this conversation goes a long way. Adopting a stance as a culturally humble and curious consultant who wants to learn from the client, rather than an expert who has the answers, will serve you well. Listen first and listen deeply to the client, seeking only to understand not to respond. This does not mean that you will not introduce perspectives or alternative frames, particularly when it seems likely that something in the client's religious or spiritual life is psychologically damaging, but this is always done tentatively and with the utmost respect for the client's belief system. Imagine the alternative in which a therapist authoritatively presents a perspective early in the counseling process around an issue where the client has held a long-standing belief, perhaps for decades. Such arrogance on the part of clinicians is, unfortunately, far too ubiquitous and rarely, if ever, effective. Clients become defensive, and the therapeutic alliance and client safety can be quickly destroyed. Effective integration work occurs when we come alongside those we are led to serve in this process, rather than when we hold the stance of expert. At the same time, there are instances where gentle perturbation of the client's cognitive schema is needed. To that end, in this chapter we explore religious coping as a framework for understanding healthy versus toxic beliefs, including those that may be imposed on an individual by their religious community, potentially constituting religious abuse.

Finally, mental health professionals in various disciplines have established competencies around psychospiritual integration (Oxhandler & Pargament, 2018) with additional efforts to develop competencies underway in other disciplines (Parker, 2019). Because this book is intended to be interdisciplinary, it is beyond the scope of our efforts here to chronicle these competencies, but it is paramount that the clinician interested in psychospiritual integration and working with issues of religious abuse be familiar with both the ethical codes of their profession, ethical decision-making models, ethical principles, and the aspirational competencies established for their profession.

## Religious Coping

Religious beliefs, practices, and experiences can provide a significant source of comfort amid distress. Ken Pargament, Professor Emeritus at Bowling Green State University, has long been a leader in the study of religious coping. He found that religious coping serves five major functions: to discover meaning, to garner control, to acquire comfort by virtue of feeling close to one's Higher Power, to achieve closeness with other people, and to transform life (Pargament, Koenig, & Perez, 2000). Religion has the potential to support each of these five functions. In the presence of religious abuse, however, there is also the potential for these five functions to be adversely affected. For example, overemphasis on a judging and wrathful God or on the sinfulness of humanity can leave people feeling either that God does not care of them or that they are unworthy of God's love, in which case they may be unable to access the comfort of feeling close to God.

Additionally, religious coping can be either positive or negative, and the use of each has distinct implications on how the individual responds to stressful circumstances (Pargament, Smith, Koenig, & Perez, 1998). Examples of positive religious coping include building a collaborative relationship with God as a partner, valuing God's love and care, having a secure relationship with God, a sense of spiritual connectedness with other people, and a view of God and world as benevolent (Pargament, Feuille, & Burdzy, 2011). This is in stark contrast with negative religious coping, which includes viewing stressors as punishment from God, passively deferring to God without taking appropriate and available action on the stressor, and attempting to cope without God's help. Such approaches are viewed as "underlying spiritual tensions and struggles within oneself, with others, and with the divine" (Pargament et al., 2011, p. 51). As may be obvious, then, religious teaching that promotes these negative religious coping strategies may have deleterious effects on one's psychology and can elevate to the level of abuse.

Additionally, as you consider the religious coping being used by the individual and whether it is adaptive or maladaptive psychologically, it is important to keep in mind that clients are working to either *develop, preserve, or transform* their religious beliefs and practices. Some clients with a religious belief system may not have developed aspects of religious coping fully and may benefit from a basic exploration of how their faith life can be adaptive and sustaining during psychological and emotional distress. Other clients have a system of religious coping but also seem to recognize in a tangible way that it is not working for them. For such clients, part of the therapy process can be exploring more explicitly what is working and not working, and what other approaches to religious coping might be available. As can be seen, clients in these first two categories approach the therapy process with an openness for new ideas and change. More challenging, however, is the client who is in a preservation stance, particularly when there are beliefs, practices, and religious coping that are psychologically maladaptive. At best, such clients present with ambivalence or mild resistance to exploring other options. At worst, however, there is a strong defensive reaction from the client, usually indicative of a fear of change and or a perceived threat in considering alternatives. Later in the book, we will discuss the use of *Motivational Interviewing* (Miller & Rollnick, 2012) to work with clients in this space. For now, however, recognizing the importance of these three client stances toward their religious beliefs, practices, experiences, and coping is critical to inform the work. We have seen, for examples, far too many clinicians take an overly confrontational and explicit approach to changing beliefs and coping strategies for a client presenting in a preservation stance, and, predictably, the outcomes are not good in these cases as the clinician occasions resistance from the client and quickly damages the therapeutic relationship.

## Healthy versus Toxic Religious Beliefs

Beginning in Chapter 2, we will be discussing and exploring many different forms of religious abuse. In many cases, these will involve overt acts by religious leaders. An often more subtle form of religious abuse occurs, however, when religious teachings fail to support wellness and optimal psychological functioning or, even worse, have deleterious effects on the psychology of congregants.

Discussion of what is healthy versus unhealthy or even toxic religious/spiritual beliefs are difficult conversations because there is wide variance in beliefs. What one person might consider toxic or abusive within a religious community might be considered good theology or sound beliefs by others. Many of the ideas represented in the table and subsequent narrative have empirical or anecdotal support as causing psychological struggles or hardships. Because it is hard for us to imagine that healthy spiritual beliefs would be iatrogenic (literally "causing illness"), these hold value for discussion and exploration. The idea here is that when religious leaders or communities promote unhealthy or toxic beliefs or practices, they are fostering *un*wellness within their communities. We provide a partial list here and will discuss these at various points throughout the book.

| *Healthy* | *Unhealthy/Toxic* |
|---|---|
| Collaborative | Controlling or deferring |
| Courage to face intrapersonal difficulties | Ways to avoid intrapersonal difficulties |
| Courage to experience and appropriately express undesirable emotions | Ways to avoid uncomfortable emotions |
| Builds bridges between people | Builds barriers between people |
| Strengthens trust in the universe | Weakens/destabilizes trust in the universe |
| Stimulates inner freedom | Weakens inner freedom/autonomy |
| Fosters personal responsibility | Diminishes personal responsibility |
| Promotes forgiveness, redemption, and grace | Fosters guilt and shame |
| Encourages acceptance of reality | Encourages denial of reality |
| Recognizes forgiveness as a process | Demands forgiveness as an event |

*Collaborative versus controlling or deferring.* This first distinction is grounded in research on religious coping (Oxhandler & Pargament, 2018). One of the overarching findings is that for individuals with a theistic belief system, those who engage in a collaborative relationship with their Higher Power, using their agency where they can and surrendering things they cannot control, tend to far better in various high stress situations. This stance is perhaps most eloquently captured in the short version of the *Serenity Prayer*, purportedly written by theologian Reinhold Niebuhr:

> God grant me the Serenity to accept the things I cannot change, Courage to change the things I can, and Wisdom to know the difference.

Serenity to accept what cannot be changed, courage to act where action steps are available, and discernment between the two stand in stark contrast to the other two coping styles described by Pargament (1997): *controlling* and *deferring*. Using the framework of the *Serenity Prayer*, a *controlling* coping style occurs when an individual believes they can change all things, leaving them with no room for the peace of accepting that some things are beyond their control. In contrast, the *deferring* strategy may include the belief that to exercise personal agency expresses a lack of faith in one's Higher Power.

Given that a collaborative stance has been shown empirically to be related to positive health and mental health outcomes (Oxhandler & Pargament, 2018), religious abuse can occur within this framework whenever spiritual teachers or leaders overemphasize either the controlling or deferring strategy. For example, within a prosperity theology, an individual might be coerced into donating more to a religious community than they can afford to do with a promise that it will be returned many times over (Jones & Woodbridge, 2011). Interestingly, this reflects, to some extent, both a controlling and a deferring strategy as the individual is trying to control how their Higher Power will treat them through their gifts, but also is deferring to the teachings of a prosperity theologist. That is, the individual comes to believe that they can control their financial success by donating to their religious community. Alternatively, an individual may be shamed when this does not occur, being told, for example, that their gifts were not returned to them many times over because they are somehow not "right" with their Higher Power. Such messages can be deeply shaming and leave an individual with pervasive feelings of inadequacy, abandonment by their Higher Power, or both (i.e., "God is not here for me because I don't deserve it").

Perhaps an even more common form of religious abuse occurs when an individual is encouraged to take a *deferring* strategy. In extreme examples, individuals may be discouraged from seeking medical support for serious medical issues, or women are told not to take action in abusive marriages but rather to "submit" to the abusive partner. We believe in the power of prayer and faith in God. At the same time, in the Muslim tradition, there is a wonderful hadith or saying of the Prophet Muhammad of a Bedouin man who was stepping away from his camel without tying it up. When the Prophet asked, "Why don't you tie down your camel?" the man answered, "Because my faith is in Allah." The Prophet replied, "Tie your camel first, and then put your trust in Allah." This, perhaps, is the essence of the collaborative coping strategy.

Another common form of religious abuse occurs when individuals are encouraged to eschew mental health support (therapy, support groups, medication, etc.) and told to instead pray away the problem. As with other examples, when the psychological challenges do not dissipate, there can be an added level of shame that somehow their prayers are wrong or not worthy of an affirmative response.

*Courage to face intrapersonal difficulties versus avoiding.* Many people struggle, at least at times, with depression, anxiety, or both. Unfortunately, however, some clergy teach that if one has sufficient faith and is right with God, such mood difficulties will never occur. Similar to the above example, such a stance can create a great deal of shame for the individual who is experiencing a dysphoric mood and, in fact, increase the feelings of hopelessness/ helplessness that often accompany depression or the fears that can drive anxiety, exacerbating the psychological symptomology. In this case, the theological teaching to turn toward one's religious beliefs and practices and away from the psychological struggles becomes a form of spiritual bypass, a term coined by John Welwood (2000) to describe the experiences of some long-term meditators who used the practice to avoid their psychological difficulties. The long version of the aforementioned Serenity Prayer includes a line that the spiritual path is of "Accepting hardship as the pathway to peace." Leaning in to the difficulties, with support as needed, is the healthy psychological path. Using religious beliefs and practices to avoid, deny, and suppress often occasions more serious mental health issues.

*Experiencing and expressing emotions versus avoidance.* Similar to mood, the healthy experience and expression of emotions is critical to mental health. It is the human condition to feel, at various times, a full range of emotions. While there are many unhealthy ways to act on these emotions, experiencing and expressing emotions in a healthy way is a foundation of mental health and should be supported and encouraged. Unfortunately, however, the message from religious leaders seems to confuse temperance with avoidance and suppression. Being slow to anger is not the same as suppressing angry feelings toward someone who hurts you. When religious teachers or leaders suggest to people that they should not feel anger, sadness, or fear or, worse, that such experiences and expressions reflect a lack of faith, congregants begin to suppress emotions or feel shame around their emotional experience, both of which are antithetical to mental health.

*Bridges versus barriers.* Compassion, including self-compassion, supports mental health. When a religious tradition teaches love and compassion for the struggles of others, including those who have been historically minoritized and oppressed, congregants develop the capacity their capacity to love and show mercy and grace to those who are oppressed. In contrast, when religious communities are built on a foundation of othering, the ongoing and ubiquitous process of determining who is in an in-group and who is in an out-group promotes judgment and condemnation, and congregants learn to operate from this judgmental stance. Such dualistic thinking does not support optimal functioning and mental health.

*Trust in the universe.* Optimal mental health functioning occurs when there is a general acceptance of *what is* that emanates from a sense of trust in a benevolent Higher Power. This sense of a benevolent Higher Power is crucial during difficult times and, in particular, during experiences that are difficult, if not impossible, to make sense of and understand. By extension, attachment and connection to a Loving Higher Power is easily translated into being loved and, by extension, being loveable. Two of the greatest existential attachment-based fears that greatly impact psychological health and relational functioning are the fear of abandonment and the fear of inadequacy. Unfortunately, some struggle with both fears (I will be abandoned because I am inadequate). These show up in relationships, including in the family of origin, where children develop core beliefs ("No one will be there for me" versus "Those around me will support me") that can become unconscious organizing beliefs that greatly impact both psychological functioning and relationships with others. Religious teachings of a Higher Power who is loving, merciful, gracious, and forgiving may reduce people's fears around this, though there is some evidence that individuals are inclined to project their family of origin on to their image of God (Clinton & Straub, 2014), suggesting that more than religious teachings are in play. In contrast, religious leaders who emphasize a malevolent Higher Power who is quick to punish, condemn, and turn from his children who stray, may occasion fears of abandonment or inadequacy, and create a culture of shame within the individual, particularly when these scripts also are being established in the family of origin.

*Forgiveness, redemption, and grace versus guilt and shame.* From a mental health perspective, spiritual precepts of forgiveness, redemption, mercy, compassion, and grace, extended both to others and to the self, are healthy. In contrast, teachings and interactions that shame and belittle congregants, by extension modeling these behaviors, lead to negative psychological outcomes. This is religion at its worst, a form of social control that cuts a wide path of wounded souls.

*Acceptance of reality.* Healthy religion and spirituality accept all that is. Most of us fall short of this mark, but being at peace with *what is* remains an aspirational goal. Drawing again from the long version of the Serenity Prayer, we find the following words:

**Taking, as He Did, This Sinful World As It Is, Not As I Would Have It.**

Much of what has been discussed previously in this section applies here. When religious teachers and leaders tell us to deny that we are depressed, deny that we are anger, deny that we are fearful, and tell us again and again that we are bad people, to the point that we no longer need others to tell us this as we tell ourselves, this is emotionally and psychologically abusive.

*Forgiveness as a process.* From a psychological standpoint, we understand forgiveness as a process. First, we have to make a decision whether we want to forgive the offending person, a process that can take substantial time as we wrestle with our natural defenses against forgiveness. If (not when) we make a decision to forgive, the practice of forgiveness also takes time (Worthington, 2019). While we believe in miracles and that it is possible for a grievance to simply be taken away by a Higher Power, the reality for the overwhelming majority is that forgiveness is a process that takes time, dedication, and work. Unfortunately, however, we have worked with many religious clients in our practice who were directed by religious teachers and leaders to simply let go of their anger, as if flipping a light switch. More times than not, this compounds the frustration and anger the person feels with shame at being unable to do what they were directed to do. Rarely have we heard a client say, "That person was wrong." Instead, what we hear is self-recrimination, loud shouts from an inner critique that laments, "What is wrong with me?" This can elevate to the level of abuse.

We close this section with a case study, a composite of a real client with identifying information changed to protect their identity:

For as long as she can remember, Mariah, a 27-year-old White female has struggled with mild to moderate depression. When in its milder form, Mariah is aware of her lethargy and "heaviness", but through a variety of wellness activities, including exercise, good diet, and a rich religious life, she is able to function well. When the depression has been at a more moderate level, however, she has struggled to focus at work and home, feels a heightened sense of anhedonia, eats less well, rarely if ever exercises, and often isolates from her religious community. Over the past year, however, beginning soon after her mother died suddenly and unexpectedly, Mariah's depression has been far worse. Mariah's relationship with her mother was complicated and the last conversation Mariah had with her mother before she died was an argument that ended when Mariah stormed out of her mother's house. She never spoke to her again as her mother died less than 72 hours later. Of particular importance in Mariah's story is that she went to her mother's house to try to repair the relationship and she was the one who found her mother dead in her bathroom floor, a victim of a massive heart attack. After that, she rarely engaged in her religious community and found herself angry at God for taking her mother so young. She also felt guilt about their last fight, even though part of her knew she was right about what they had been arguing over. She was not eating healthy and was aware, at times, of eating to excess to "stuff" painful emotions. She also was rarely exercising and had gained substantive weight over the past year. She had gotten a poor performance evaluation at work and knew she was in jeopardy of losing her job. She began isolating from her religious community and from her close friends. One close friend, knowing the salience of her religious identity historically encourages her to talk to her clergy. She is hesitant, given her anger at God, but also knows that she is not doing well and that she needs help, so she goes to her clergy. Her clergy listened to her for a few minutes and then said, "You know, Mariah, your mother is in a better place, so you need not be sad that she is gone. And, perhaps, God just needed another angel and you know that God knows best.

I want you to go home and pray, earnestly, every day at least 3–4 times per day. Pray with the knowledge that God will heal your sadness if you only ask." Mariah acquiesced in the moment that she would do just that but had to stop her car on the drive home because she was so angry and crying so hard.

What becomes complicated in these situations is that there are many who would argue that the clergy's words were theologically sound, that earnest prayer for healing is the answer. For Mariah, however, it was abusive. How are we comfortable saying that? Because Mariah told one of us (CC) in her therapy that she felt abused and traumatized by the words of her clergy. She exhibited clear symptoms of Post-Traumatic Stress Disorder, including the characteristic triad of rumination and re-experiencing (Mariah reported that she could not get the clergy's voice and words out of her head), avoidance (Mariah indicated a number of unhealthy avoidant coping behaviors just, as she said, "to get to the next day"), and increased arousal (Mariah reported "coming out of my skin almost all the time"). Maria attributed her struggles not solely to the clergy as she recognized the trauma of her mother's unexpected death. When she presented in counseling, however, she felt totally lost as she had tried to do as her clergy directed, but would quickly experience trauma symptoms when she tried to pray. It is important to note here that we do not question that the *intent* of the clergy was to be helpful, but the *impact* of this conversation was quite harmful to Mariah. Further, the harm included the psychological, emotional, and spiritual realms of Mariah's life. Prior to her mother's death, Mariah had struggled with a sense that neither God nor anyone else was really there for her, a fear that she had never felt safe enough to share with anyone else. This fear was exacerbated first with her mother's sudden and untimely death and then again by essentially feeling dismissed by a clergy member who didn't seem to care enough to spend time with her in her pain. That is, the experience with her clergy member became another source of abandonment. And, since she had been taught from an early age that clergy were "closer to God than other humans", a message her mother gave her often when telling her that she should not question the clergy, this re-triggered the abandonment. By directing her to use solely prayer to cure her depression, which appears to have endogenous roots exacerbated by the death of her mother, the clergy encouraged a deferring strategy, which negatively played in to a negative internal script that Mariah had that she had no agency in her life, perhaps part of what left her feeling hopeless and part of what was driving her depression.

This list is not meant to be exhaustive. As you will see throughout this book, religious abuse comes from behaviors that are psychologically, emotionally, physically, and sexually abusive as well as from teaching and dogma that are oppressive and psychologically damaging. Throughout this book, we will explore not only the narratives of the occurrence of religious abuse, but also explore the impact of such abuse. In some instances, clients come to us aware of negative experiences within their religious communities but unaware that they have been abused and are having logical reactions to a traumatic experience. We will unpack some of these scenarios and discuss not only what happens but how it tends to impact the congregant who is abused. As Hellen Keller once wrote, "Although the world is full of suffering, it is full also of the overcoming of it", so we also will explore the process of healing from religious abuse, a path that is complex and nuanced for therapists and clients alike.

## Assessing/Broaching Religion and Spirituality

There is an old adage that religion and politics should never be discussed in mixed company, the dated term *mixed* company referring simply to situations in which you do not already know the belief system of those in the gathering. While this may be sage advice in social situations, understanding if, when, and how to broach topics of religion and spirituality is critical for counselors. Given the sensitive and highly personal nature of religion and spirituality, though, conversations can be delicate. In some cases, clients can be eager to discuss their religion or spirituality if they are looking to develop or transform their spirituality in some way. In other cases, however, clients can be hesitant to talk about their religious or spiritual life, borne of a fear that the therapist might judge them or try to change them, or because they are struggling with strong undesirable emotions around their religious experience.

How, then, does the therapist best broach this topic with clients? While there are many quantitative and qualitative assessments available to assess religiosity and spirituality (Harper, Gill, & Dailey, 2020), most of these are beyond the scope of initial intakes. In fact, overemphasizing religion and spirituality in an initial assessment could be off-putting or even offensive to some clients and damage the therapeutic relationship and the client's sense of safety.

Initially, we recommend a very simple assessment of two questions that could easily be included in an intake form or asked of every client as part of an intake interview. The sequence of questions looks like this:

|  | Not at All Important |  | Very Important |
|---|---|---|---|
| How important is religion/spirituality to you? | 1   2 | 3 | 4   5 |
| Do you want to talk about your religion/spirituality in therapy? |  | No | Yes |

Optionally, you could consider a third open-ended question such as "What, if anything, do you want me to know about your religion/spirituality?"

although this can also emerge organically through conversations. These questions yield a wealth of initial information. First, we recommend the use of the hyphenated "religion/spirituality" to recognize the different language that people use. Interestingly, it is not uncommon for a client to either circle or strike through one of these two words, showing a language preference that likely has meaning for them. In fact, we have seen paper intake forms with one of these two words marked through so fiercely that the page was, in fact, torn by the action. Some people have a strong preference for one of the two terms, and some have a strong negative connotation of one of the two words. This format allows for expression of that.

Responses on these two questions can yield a lot of initial information that guides the early therapy process. For example, a client who responds with a high score (4 or 5) and "Yes" to the second question is inviting broaching this topic in an initial session. You can explore with the client whether the presenting issue is a religious/spiritual problem, such as religious abuse, or whether they see the presenting issue as separate from their religious/spiritual life, but want you to know that religion or spirituality is a salient identity for them. Similarly, a clear-cut "1" and "No" response likely indicates that the client does not view either religion or spirituality as relevant to their presenting issue AND that the religion/spiritual identity is less salient for them in general. In these instances, a competent therapist proceeds with good therapy without asking further questions or broaching the religion/spirituality topic unless it later becomes relevant in some way.

Additionally, however, there are some interesting combinations of responses that warrant mentioning. We have seen a "1" and "Yes" response many times from clients. Given the invitation to broach the topic in their response to the second question, we explore with curiosity the meaning these responses hold for the client. In many instances, this simply reflects that the client has not historically been religious or spiritual but is experiencing a longing to develop their spirituality, whether within organized religion or not. Another common response, one more germane to the topic of religious abuse, occurs when a client responds with a "5" and "No" pattern. Initially, we honor the client's request not to talk about religion/spirituality in the therapy room. Once a sufficient therapeutic alliance has been built, however, typically within two to four sessions, we recommend broaching with permission:

> There was something on your intake that is curious to me and out of that curiosity and caring for you, part of me wants to ask you more about it, but another part wants to honor that you indicated a preference not to talk about it.

Interestingly, a short pause here often leads a client to say, "Oh, about my religion/spirituality. Well, that's about...", which gives you a greater sense of the meaning behind their response pattern. In other instance, no response from the client can prompt a question:

Since I am unsure how to proceed, I want to be respectful here. Would it be ok if I asked you just a little about your religion and spirituality?

Asking permission, a skill that emerged from *Motivational Interviewing* (Miller & Rollnick, 2013), leaves the client in the one-up power position and is deeply respectful of the client. The combination of humble curiosity and asking permission often creates enough safety for the client to speak to the meaning of their response. In some cases, this is simply a clarification, such as "My religion is very important to me, but my spiritual life is good and, yet, my anxiety is unabated. I really want to tackle this from a psychological perspective," which leads the therapist to let go of further exploration of religion/spirituality, perhaps with a statement such as "Oh, ok, I get that. Unless I hear something different from you, then, we will honor together your request and focus on this solely at a psychological level. If that changes for you, please let me know."

In other cases, however, this "5" and "No" combination represents something different. We commonly hear things like "Well, I'm (marginalized religion) and I'm concerned that you won't understand or will judge me for that" or "I've heard in my church that secular therapists sometimes try to change people's religion and I have no interest in changing anything about my religion, so I don't want to talk about it." In these instances, based solely on extra-therapy experiences, the client does not feel safe integrating their religious or spiritual lives into the counseling process. In either the former case, where the client has experienced marginalization because of religion or spirituality, or the latter case, where the client wishes to preserve their current beliefs and practices, the critical work is creating safety in the therapeutic process by validating and normalizing their concerns and your earnest desire to be nonjudgmental and respect any aspect of their lives that they choose to preserve, highlighting the ethical principle of autonomy which will be explored more fully in Section "Defining Religion and Spirituality", where we discuss ethical codes and ethical principles critical to competent care of individuals who have experienced religious abuse.

## Conclusion

While there is much that is beautiful within religious communities, throughout this book, we will explore the phenomenon of religious abuse, the sequelae of such abuse, and the path to healing. In this chapter, we have primarily discussed psychospiritual integration within the therapy process and provided some preliminary information about religious coping and belief systems that are associated with adaptive and maladaptive psychological functioning. In Chapter 2, we turn our attention more explicitly to the experience of religious abuse.

# References

Cashwell, C. S., & Pulgar, C. (2019, June). *Imposing, demeaning, or ignoring: Client experiences of therapists who are insensitive to religious and spiritual beliefs.* Association for Spiritual, Ethical, and Religious Values in Counseling Annual Conference, Colorado Springs, CO.

Cashwell, C. S., & Young, J. S. (Eds.) (2020). *Integrating spirituality in counseling: A guide to competent practice* (3rd ed.). Alexandria, VA: American Counseling Association.

Clinton, T., & Straub, J. (2014). *God attachment: Why you believe, act, and feel the way you do about God.* Brentwood, TN: Howard Books.

Gill, C. S., Harper, M. C., & Dailey, S. F. (2020). Assessing the spiritual and religious domains. In C. S. Cashwell & J. S. Young (Eds.), *Integrating spirituality and religion into counseling: A guide to competent practice* (pp. 165–189). Alexandria, VA: American Counseling Association.

Harris, S. (2014). *Waking up: A guide to spirituality without religion.* New York: Simon & Shuster.

James, W. (2012). *The varieties of religious experience* (M. Bradley, Ed.). Oxford: Oxford University Press.

Jones, D., & Woodbridge, R. (2011). *Health, wealth & happiness: Has the prosperity gospel overshadowed the gospel of Christ?* Grand Rapids, MI: Kregel.

Jung, C. G. (1960). *The structure and dynamics of the psych.* London: Routledge.

Klotz, N. D. (2001). *The hidden gospel: Decoding the spiritual message of the Aramaic Jesus.* Wheaton, IL: Quest books.

Koenig, H., King, D., & Carson, V. B. (2012). *Handbook of religion and health* (2nd ed.). New York: Oxford University Press.

Miller, W. R., & Rollnick, S. (2012). *Motivational interviewing: Helping people change.* Guilford press.

Oxhandler, H. K., & Pargament, K. I. (2018). Measuring religious and spiritual competence across helping professions: Previous efforts and future directions. *Spirituality in Clinical Practice, 5,* 120–132.

Pargament, K. I. (1997). *The psychology of religion and coping: Theory, research, practice.* New York: Guilford.

Pargament, K. I., Feuille, M., & Burdzy, D. (2011). The brief RCOPE: Current psychometric status of a short measure of religious coping. *Religions, 21,* 51–76.

Pargament, K. I., Koenig, H. G., & Perez, L. M. (2000). The many methods of religious coping: Development and initial validation of the RCOPE. *Journal of Clinical Psychology, 56,* 519–543.

Pargament, K. I., Smith, B. W., Koenig, H. G., & Perez, L. (1998). Patterns of positive and negative religious coping with major life stressors. *Journal for the Scientific Study of Religion, 374,* 710–724.

Parker, J. S. (2019). Spiritual and religious multicultural practice competencies: A partial replication study with school psychologists. *School Psychology Forum, 13,* 53–73.

Pew Research Center. (2015). *Religious landscape study.* Pew Forum. https://www.pewforum.org/religious-landscape-study/

Welwood, J. (2000). *Toward a psychology of awakening: Buddhism, psychotherapy, and the path of personal and spiritual transformation.* Boston, MA: Shambhala.

Wilber, K. (2000). *Integral psychology: Consciousness, spirit, psychology, therapy*. Boston, MA: Shambhala.

Worthington, E. L., & Wade, N. G. (Eds.) (2019). *Handbook of forgiveness* (2nd ed.). New York: Routledge.

Young, J. S., & Cashwell, C. S. (2020). Integrating spirituality and religion into counseling: An introduction. In C. S. Cashwell & J. S. Young (Eds.), *Integrating spirituality and religion into counseling: A guide to competent practice* (pp. 3–29). Alexandria, VA: American Counseling Association.

# 2 Defining Religious Abuse

As discussed in Chapter 1, it is imperative for therapists to broach the subject of religion or spirituality as part of a client's worldview or cultural experience. As part of this assessment, the therapist must be prepared for whatever information the client presents in response. When counselors gather religious/ spiritual information as part of the counseling process, many clients will disclose positive and supportive experiences. When a client discloses a supportive religious experience, this may be used as a strength or source of support in the therapeutic process and may be very helpful for the client. If this relationship with the sacred has been positive and nurturing for their client, it can drive healing and be a grounding force (Simonic, Mandelj, & Novsak, 2013).

Unfortunately, however, clients may also disclose different experiences that reveal a shadow side to organized religion. The potential for both positive and negative influences of a religious worldview are apparent in Competency 11 of the Association for Spiritual, Ethical, and Religious Values in Counseling (ASERVIC), Competencies for Addressing Spiritual and Religious Issues in Counseling, which states, "When making a diagnosis, the professional counselor recognizes that the client's spiritual and/or religious perspectives can a) enhance well-being; b) contribute to client problems; and/or c) **exacerbate symptoms**" (Cashwell & Watts, 2010, p. 5).

This "exacerbation of symptoms" as a result of a client's involvement with religion may show in a wide variety of ways along a continuum of harm. For some clients, negative religious experiences may contribute to their problems or exacerbate symptoms in a way that suggest that the religious experience is detrimental to the individual. For a subset of these individuals, the negative religious/spiritual experience may be so severe as to be considered *religious abuse*. It is important for counselors to feel competent in addressing religious experiences across this positive/negative spectrum. This includes understanding how to use a client's positive experiences as a source of support and coping as well as knowing how to address negative religious experiences that may present or emerge as a presenting issue or stressor.

Religious abuse includes mental, physical, sexual, and/or emotional abuse that happens within a religious context or setting, often resulting in experiences of trauma for the individual (Cashwell & Swindle, 2018; Swindle, 2017). The key here is to understand the impact that may occur when adding the element of religion, or the sacred, to an experience of abuse. The term "religious abuse" is often used interchangeably with "spiritual abuse," and for the purposes of this book, the term "religious abuse" will be the primary term. The rationale for this is that, although there is an inherent spiritual connection to most experiences within a religious institution, the content of this book will focus on experiences within religious organizations or institutions. In addition, although religious abuse may occur within any religious organization, and the content will include potential experiences in a wide variety of religious traditions, the primary focus of the information will be experiences within churches that identify as Christian.

Following a thorough review of the interdisciplinary religious abuse literature, three broad categories or types of religious abuse emerged, particularly those that occur within mainstream Christian churches. The categories are not mutually exclusive and experiences of religious abuse may coexist in multiple categories or overlap into multiple categories. The three broad categories of religious abuse described to this point in the scholarly literature are as follows:

1 Abuse perpetrated by religious leadership, typically an individual leader
2 Abuse perpetrated by a religious group, directed either toward an individual or toward a group of people
3 Abuse in which the abuse itself has a religious component to it (Swindle, 2017).

These three categories capture the wide range and variety of experiences that may fall under the umbrella of religious abuse.

## Abuse Perpetrated by Religious Leadership

Abuse perpetrated by religious leadership includes physical (such as a Sunday school teacher who physically harms students), sexual (such as youth minister who sexually abuses a member of the youth group), and emotional abuse (such as a minister who refuses to marry an interracial couple) where the perpetrator is a person in an officially named position of religious authority or leadership. This is typically a pastor or member of the clergy, although it may also include other religious authority figures in the church, such as deacons, elders, or small group or Sunday school teachers. The vast majority of literature in this category addresses the sexual abuse crisis in the Catholic Church (Doyle, 2003, 2006; Farrell, 2004; Goldner, 2004; Hogan, 2011; Rossetti, 1995; Saradjian & Nobus, 2003), although sexual abuse perpetrated by a clergy member is certainly not limited to Catholicism (Farrell, 2004), and religious leaders can abuse in many ways beyond sexual abuse.

One of the key elements of this category is that the abuser is seen or held forth as a representative of God. There is great power that comes with this representation, and power differentials are a component of all abuse situations. Sacred power is inherently built into the concept of a person who is God's representative on earth. Some denominations have specific theologies that espouse those in positions of religious authority know God better than others and have a closer relationship to God. It can be very difficult for those who believe in God to feel empowered to challenge those who are held up as God's representative on earth.

An additional significant issue that may arise in religious abuse that is perpetrated by Christian religious leadership is the potential for the victim to conflate the abuser with God (Doyle, 2006; Farrell, 2004; Redmond, 1996; Rossetti, 1995). When someone who is God's spokesperson or representative harms or abuses you, it is not a big leap to wonder if God is abusing you, or at least endorsing the abuse you are experiencing.

In addition to the conflation of the abuser with God, there may also be a conflation of the abuser with all religion or all churches. Victims may believe that this person represents what all religious leaders are like, resulting in a spiritual mistrust of all religious leaders and religious systems, and separate the victims from their current or potential spiritual communities of support (Doyle, 2003; Redmond, 1996; Rossetti, 1995).

### *Counselor Implications*

This may also be an important concept for therapists who are treating victims of religious abuse. A client's conflation of the abuser with God may create challenges for the counselor. If the counselor is religious, they may notice an internal desire to disentangle this conflation and defend God or to convince the client that there are other religious experiences available to them. In these instances, it is extremely important for the counselor to adhere to ASERVIC Competency 4 "The professional counselor continuously evaluates the influence of his or her own spiritual and/or religious beliefs and values on the client and the counseling process" (ASERVIC, 2009). This self-awareness and reflection could help to head off the tendency of helping professionals who are religious to defend God or to try to convince the client that "God isn't really like that" (Redmond, 1996, p. 41). At the other end of the religious spectrum, counselors who are anti-religion in their beliefs also need to engage in this self-reflection to ensure they are not influencing clients away from religious systems or beliefs due to their own biases.

## Abuse Perpetrated by a Religious Group

The next category of religious abuse is that which is perpetrated more broadly by a religious group or community, or a person who is representing the religion or religious groups. Abuse in which the perpetrator is a religious group includes situations where the abuser(s) may target and exclude a marginalized population and use religious teachings or theology selectively in order to oppress, sending the overt or covert message that "you may not be a part of our group." The abuser may be one person claiming to represent an entire group, or it may be an actual group of people or religious system that is oppressing either an individual or a population of people. This type of abuse creates a "legitimized inequality" (Greene, 2013, p. 41) as the religious abuser seeks to *other* a marginalized group or member of a marginalized group. The abuse is experienced as coming from the system rather than an identified individual within the system.

For example, multiple authors have discussed the impact of religious abuse on the LGTBQ+ (Lesbian, Gay, Transgender, Bisexual, Queer plus) population (Foster, Bowland & Vosler, 2015; Greene, 2013; Lucies & Yick, 2007; Super & Jacobson, 2011; Wood & Conley, 2014). Foster et al. (2015) found that "the homonegativity perpetuated in many Christian churches makes it difficult for LG Christians to retain their religion/spirituality while embracing their sexual orientation" (p. 191). The religious othering experienced by members of the LGBTQ population often sends messages that convey that this population is evil or less loved by God, a message that may be internalized by an individual in this group (Alison, 2001; Super & Jacobson, 2011). Some lesbian and gay Christians describe difficulty in finding a safe spiritual community or choose to separate from their spiritual community (Foster et al., 2015; Super & Jacobson, 2011).

Another example of this category would be a woman who is exiled or ostracized by the entire church or church members because she chose to leave an abusive marriage. Some churches practice "church discipline" in this way and have been known to have meetings about a particular member and direct the entire group that they are not to associate with this person until they have "repented" and come back to the church and their marriage. This type of abuse could then be acted out within the church building or outside the church walls. In this situation, a church member refusing to talk to this person in the grocery store would be considered rude in most circumstances. However, the fact that this is a result of a directive from the religious system, intending to send a message that the shunning was a result of the woman's moral failing in some way adds the element of religious abuse.

There is an inherent message of superiority or "better than" that is sent in this category of abuse by the religious group or representative of the religious group. This message is grounded in and justified by the notion that God is siding with the religious group, which can heighten and embolden the oppression and hate speech which can emerge. In this category, the power of the sacred can be twisted into a weapon of oppression and justification for self-righteousness and the exclusion of some from the religious system.

This type of abuse perpetrated by a religious group has also been seen as some religious systems have promoted racism in both macro (e.g., a governmental structure of apartheid) and micro (e.g., a pastor who refuses to perform a marriage ceremony for an interracial couple) contexts.

## Abuse with a Religious Component

Finally, some forms of religious abuse appear to involve a direct connection to something spiritual or religious wherein the abuse itself is a result of religious belief or has a religious theological element tied to the actual abuse. Although it can be argued that the other two types of religious abuse (abuse perpetrated by religious leadership or abuse perpetrated by a religious group) have an inherent religious component as they are originating from a person or people connected to a religious group, this third type of religious abuse involves an overt tie to religious belief (Swindle, 2017).

For example, Bottoms et al. (2015) provided an example of parents who physically abuse their children and justify it by telling the child they must have the devil or evil beaten out of them. The action of the physical abuse itself, while horrific, would not be categorized as religious abuse without the stated motivation of beating the evil out of the child due to the parents' interpretation of their religious teachings. The message sent to the child is that this abuse is part of their religion and has an overt connection to God.

Other examples include domestic violence situations in which the husband justifies beating his wife because of religious beliefs (Simonic, Mandelj, & Novsak, 2013). Some Christians may interpret the biblical concept of submission to mean that women should not seek help if they experience intimate partner violence and that they are not allowed to question their husbands' authority. In cases such as these, this theological interpretation may drive both the actions of the abuser to abuse and the actions of the victim to remain in an unsafe relationship, believing the abuse to be God-ordained.

Other forms of religious abuse that include a religious or sacred element include a sexual abuser, clergy, or, otherwise, someone who uses a spiritual element to perpetrate the abuse. For example, the predator might tell a child that "God wants you to do this," or "You will go to Hell if you tell anyone about this." The sacred element has the potential to amplify the power differential or perpetuate the secrecy and shame of the abuse. Another example is a clergy who financially abuses a congregant by promising favor with God if the person will make a substantial financial contribution to the church, where the abuser manipulates someone's desire for a spiritual connection for the abuser's own gain.

When conceptualizing the three broad categories of religious abuse – (1) abuse perpetrated by religious leadership, typically an individual leader, (2) abuse perpetrated by a religious group, directed either toward an individual or toward a group of people, and (3) abuse in which the abuse itself has a religious component to it – it is important to keep in mind that these three categories are not mutually exclusive and often overlap each other. It is possible for a specific experience of religious abuse to fall into one, two, or even all three categories.

## Application Exercise

To which of the categories does each of the following examples of religious abuse belong? Keep in mind that each example may fall into multiple categories.

1 A pastor comes to visit a 36-year-old woman whose husband has just died after a two-year battle with cancer. At one point in the visit, the pastor tells the woman that she and her husband must have had a lapse in faith or he would have been healed.
2 A 23-year-old gay man accepts his parents' invitation to attend their new church. During the sermon, the pastor calls him out by name and asks him to come to the front of the church so that the church can pray for him to change his "abominable ways." Later, his parents share with him that they had sought counseling from this pastor to understand his sexuality and that the pastor had suggested they invite him to church.
3 On youth Sunday, a 17-year-old teenage girl volunteers to deliver the sermon. The male youth minister agrees, but later tells her that the church staff has discussed it and that she cannot deliver the sermon for youth Sunday because it would not be appropriate for the men of the church to "sit under the teachings of a female."
4 An elderly woman is routinely pressured by her pastor to sign over her savings to the church and to change her will to leave all her money to the church. The pastor consistently says, "This is what God wants. He told me to ask you for this gift to his service."
5 A man is abusive to his wife. He often apologizes, saying, "I'm so sorry, but you know it's not really my fault. If you would just be more submissive, like those wives in the Bible the way you are supposed to be, it would be so much easier for me."

## References

Alison, J. (2001). *Faith beyond resentment: Fragments Catholic and gay*. London: Darton, Longman and Todd; Crossroad.

Association for Spiritual, Ethical and Religious Values in Counseling. (2009). *Spiritual competencies: Competencies for addressing spiritual and religious issues in counseling*. Retrieved April 8, 2015, from http://www.aservic.org/wp-content/uploads/2010/04/Spiritual-Competencies-Printer-friendly1.pdf

Bottoms, B. L., Goodman, G. S., Tolou-Shams, M., Diviak, K. R., & Shaver, P. R. (2015). Religion-related child maltreatment: A profile of cases encountered by legal and social service agencies. *Behavioral Sciences & The Law, 33*, 561–579. doi: 10.1002/bsl.2192

Cashwell, C., & Swindle, P. (2018). When religion hurts: Supervising cases of religious abuse. *The Clinical Supervisor, 37*, 182–203. (invited publication)

Cashwell, C. S., & Watts, R. E. (2010). The new ASERVIC competencies for addressing spiritual and religious issues in counseling. *Counseling and Values, 55*(1), 2–5.

Doyle, T. (2003). Roman Catholic clericalism, religious duress, and clergy sex abuse. *Pastoral Psychology, 51*, 189–231.

Doyle, T. P. (2006). Clericalism: Enabler of clergy sexual abuse. *Pastoral Psychology, 54*, 189–213. doi: 10.1007/s11089-006-6323-x.

Farrell, D. (2004). An historical viewpoint of sexual abuse perpetrated by clergy and religious. *Journal of Religion & Abuse, 6*(2), 41–80.

Foster, K. A., Bowland, S. E., & Vosler, A. N. (2015). All the pain along with all the joy: Spiritual resilience in lesbian and gay Christians. *American Journal of Community Psychology, 55*, 191–201. doi: 10.1007/s10464-015-9704-4

Goldner, V. (2004). Introduction—the sexual-abuse crisis and the Catholic church: Gender, sexuality, power and discourse. *Studies in Gender and Sexuality, 5*(1), 1–9.

Greene, B. (2013). The use and abuse of religious beliefs in dividing and conquering between socially marginalized groups: The same-sex marriage debate. *Psychology of Sexual Orientation and Gender Diversity, 1*, 35–44.

Hogan, L. (2011). Clerical and religious child abuse: Ireland and beyond. *Theological Studies, 72*, 170–186.

Lucies, C., & Yick, A. (2007). Images of gay men's experiences with antigay abuse: Object relations theory reconceptualized. *Journal of Theory Construction & Testing, 11*(2), 55–62.

Redmond, S. A. (1996). God died and nobody gave a funeral. *Pastoral Psychology, 45*(1), 41–47

Rossetti, S. J. (1995). The impact of child sexual abuse on attitudes toward God and the Catholic church. *Child Abuse & Neglect, 19*(12), 1469–1481.

Saradjian, A., & Nobus, D. (2003). Cognitive distortions of religious professionals who sexually abuse children. *Journal of Interpersonal Violence, 18*(8), 905–923.

Simonič, B., Mandelj, T. R., & Novsak, R. (2013). Religious-related abuse in the family. *Journal of Family Violence, 28*, 339–349

Super, J. T., & Jacobson, L. (2011). Religious abuse: Implications for counseling lesbian, gay, bisexual, and transgender individuals. *Journal of LGBT Issues in Counseling, 5*(3–4), 180–196. doi: 10.1080/15538605.2011.632739

Swindle, P. J. (2017). *A twisting of the sacred: The lived experience of religious abuse.* The University of North Carolina at Greensboro, ProQuest Dissertations Publishing. 10264116.

Wood, A. W. & Conley, A. H. (2014). Loss of religious or spiritual identities among the LGBT population. *Counseling and Values, 59*, 95–111.

# 3 Common Experiences of Victims of Religious Abuse

When counselors work with presentations of religious abuse, it can be helpful to understand some common emotional and psychological experiences of their clients. It can be helpful in assessing and naming the experience for clients, and also helpful to the clients to process and begin healing from the abuse. In this chapter we will discuss common experiences such as feelings of betrayal and powerlessness, grief and loss, and experiences of manipulation, trauma, marginalization and isolation, feeling devalued or worthless (rules over people), and existential crisis.

## Betrayal

One of the most pervasive and powerful emotions that many people who have experienced religious abuse report is betrayal. Finkelhor and Browne (1985) describe the betrayal dynamic as the realization of the victim that they have been harmed by someone they had depended on and deeply trusted. It is not only that they have experienced harm, but it is that the harm came from someone or something important to them and that they had specifically trusted.

Therefore, it makes sense that victims of religious abuse would experience feelings of betrayal. "Trust" is a key component of many religious systems. Those who participate are often invited to become a part of their group by reporting their trust in the common beliefs of the group. Many religious people feel their religion and religious beliefs guide their lives, so it is often a system on which they depend and where they believe they will be supported. It may feel like the ultimate betrayal that someone or a system they trusted and depended on for spiritual guidance or support has caused them harm (Bottoms et al., 2015; Doyle, 2006; Farrell, 2004; Gavrielides, 2012; Pargament, Murray-Swank, & Mahoney, 2008; Swindle, 2017).

The source of the betrayal may take many forms. Victims of religious abuse report feeling betrayed by the church leadership, the other church members whom they may have considered friends, their family, the system, the theology, and even God.

## Common Experiences of Victims of Religious Abuse 33

A unique component of this betrayal dynamic as it pertains to religious abuse is the possibility for the abuse and those perpetrating the abuse to be conflated with God, and therefore for the victim to feel betrayed by God. As described in Chapter 2 as one of the broad categories of religious abuse, when the abuser is in an official capacity in the system (a member of the clergy or designated church leader), that person is often seen as a representative of God on earth (Farrell, 2004; Rossetti, 1995), or at least called or placed by God (Doyle, 2003). In these instances, the betrayal may be felt doubly as the victim has been betrayed by the human factor, but also by God who is represented in the human (Redmond, 1996). Among the many other aspects of confusion and betrayal in abusive situations, it is also normal for victims of religious abuse to ask questions such as "How could God let this happen? What did I do wrong?" Reflecting and normalizing questions such as these and normalizing feelings of betrayal can be a very powerful part of the therapeutic process for clients.

The betrayal may also be perceived as coming from other church members. Sometimes fellow congregants act as the abuser as discussed in the second category of types of religious discussed in Chapter 2. Sometimes the people in the system shelter or cover for the abuser and undermine the experiences of the victim. In these cases, not only has the church failed to protect the victim, they may also protect the abuser. Similar to how some victims of incest feel betrayed by the non-offending parent for not protecting them, it is normal for victims of religious abuse to feel multiple layers of betrayal to include others in the system who prioritized the protection of an abusive leader over the protection of a fellow church member (Celano et al., 1996).

Clients may also present with feelings of betrayal from their family members who they believe chose the abusive system over them. Several participants in the study of Swindle (2017) reported feeling that their family has chosen the church or a religiously abusive person over them, and that this felt like a strong betrayal. Examples of this include families who maintain contact and a relationship with an abusive spouse who used theology to justify the abuse or parents who disown a child who is a member of the LGBTQ+ (Lesbian, Gay, Bisexual, Transgender, Queer+) community. These clients may feel their own family has chosen an abuser or an abusive theology over a relationship with them, or even over their own safety. Connected to this, clients may express feeling betrayed by the very theology to which they once (and may still) subscribe. Clients may express having been very committed to their beliefs and have now experienced those beliefs being used against them (Swindle, 2017).

### *Existential Crisis*

It is also quite normal to see questions such as these contribute to a questioning of meaning or an existential crisis. For many, their religion and/or their faith have/has been what has given meaning and purpose to their life, so experiences that create doubt around that meaning and purpose can be jarring. Some clients are able to separate their experiences in the system from their belief, and some do not (Swindle, 2017). Those who do not may enter into a period of deconstruction of their faith and the system. For some who have been a part of a system that promised certainty, the doubt and betrayal are very disconcerting and may contribute to experiences of depression and anxiety.

For those who continue to have religious beliefs despite the harm they have endured, this can be a confusing time of figuring out where they fit in. Some may choose to stay in the system in which the harm occurred. In these situations, counselors should be very aware of their own reactions and bias and provide space to clients rather than imposing their own agendas. Some clients may leave the system in which the harm occurred, but seek out another religious system (Swindle, 2017). In these situations, there may be existential questions and struggles, and grief at the loss of community.

## *Grief/Loss/Isolation*

Experiences of religious abuse often result in many losses. As described above regarding feelings of betrayal, clients who have experienced religious abuse may have lost their relationships with family members, their religious leaders who they may have revered and trusted, their religious community and connected friendships, and their own beliefs.

The loss of relationships with family members may be the choice of the client, or the family member may have cut off a relationship with the client. Either way, this can be a very complicated loss and additional trauma to an already difficult experience. The lack of support from a family member may cause the client to question the reality or severity of the abuse and may cause self-blame.

The same may be said for the loss of the religious community and connected relationships and friendships. Sometimes victims of religious abuse choose to leave the religious system, and sometimes they are forced out by the system, which may be a form of abuse itself. For some people, their entire social world may have revolved around their church, and losing this can feel incredibly isolating. Some may stay in their religious communities and yet feel a shift in their role and acceptance there. The same inclinations that lead systems to protect the abuser rather than the abused may also result in stigmatizing and scapegoating the victim rather than addressing the abuse in their midst (Bailie, 2004; Finkelhor, 1987). This loss of support from those most important to the client may compound the trauma they are already feeling. In a time when they need support the most, those closest to them may withdraw the support and seem to side with those who harmed them (Swindle, 2017).

Naming these losses and doing active grief work with clients is often a critical part of the healing journey in the therapeutic process. These feelings of isolation and marginalization may be a result of the abuse or may be the abuse itself.

## Powerlessness

Another potent possible experience of those abused by religion is feelings of powerlessness. Power is a dynamic at play in any abusive relationship, and for people who believe in God, there is nothing more powerful than God (Farrell, 2004). Believing that your abuser(s) has/have been empowered by God may amplify the lack of power, voice, and agency in instances of religious abuse. Connected to the feelings of betrayal, a person's religion is "supposed to be" an all-powerful comfort and sanctuary, so when the opposite is experienced, it may feel as if that power has been turned on the client in a magnified way. Those in high control and abusive religious environments are often taught to surrender any power they have and are not allowed to question the authority that God has put in place (Doyle, 2003; Hogan, 2011; Oakley & Kinmond, 2014). This may even be a part of the grooming of the victim. For abuse to continue and to survive, it must have a victim who feels powerless, so what greater power can an abuser have than to convince a victim that God is on the side of the abuser? Clients may present with a lack of trust in themselves and their own experiences, and may continue to be hesitant to question the power and authority of the system in which they experienced their abuse. There may also be blame turned inward on many levels, including the idea that "I must have deserved it, if an all powerful God allowed it."

### *Manipulation of the Sacred to Control*

The power dynamics described above put a religious abuser in a perfect position to use elements of the sacred to control their victim(s). There is so much power in invoking the sacred or the name of God. Several participants in Swindle's (2017) research study on religious abuse described feeling manipulated by their abuser's use of religion and the sacred to control them, including feeling pressured/manipulated to stay in an abusive relationship, financial manipulation, manipulated regarding the use of psychotropic medication, and manipulated by theology to limit areas of service in a religious system. Clients may describe feeling that their abuser was misusing their power or theology to control them or to make them doubt themselves.

## Rules over People

For some people who experience this kind of manipulation and control, they can receive the message that the "rules" matter more than people, including themselves. One participant in Swindle's (2017, p. 116) study on experiences of religious abuse who had experienced domestic violence reported about her church: "Literally if I had followed their rules I would be dead." Similarly, members of marginalized communities such as the LGBTQIA+ community describe such feelings when their families choose to cut off a relationship with them due to the rules of their religious community or a woman being told she cannot serve as a minister due to the rule of no women being allowed to speak in church. These kinds of experiences can contribute to the client feeling devalued and worthless when the rule is held out as more important than their safety or ability to have a relationship with their family. The individual is seen only through the lens of a rigid rule rather than the rule being interpreted through the lens of a human experience.

*Trauma*

It is also important to note that experiences of religious abuse are often experienced as trauma. In the therapeutic fields, the term "religious trauma" may be used to describe the same phenomena described in this book. All of the common experiences described so far in this chapter may be experienced as traumatic. Clients may report feeling trauma for the losses they have endured, for the deep betrayal of their trust and vulnerability, and for the isolation and loss of control they have experienced. This may show as typical symptoms of post-traumatic stress disorder which include distressing memories or nightmares, dissociation, psychological distress when exposed to cues/triggers, avoidance of triggers or reminders, negative emotional states, and hypervigilance (American Psychological Association, 2013), or it may show up as a variety of other mental health symptoms including symptoms of depression and anxiety. The use of the word "trauma" may be comforting to a client (Swindle, 2017), but, at the very least, a trauma-informed approach to therapy may be beneficial to the client.

## Conclusion

Although there are a wide variety of ways religious abuse may happen, there are several common themes that often run through the individual experiences of religious abuse. These themes include feelings of betrayal, existential crisis, grief, loss, isolation, feelings of powerlessness and loss of control, feeling devalued as the rule is valued over the person, and experiences of trauma. This is not a fully comprehensive list, and there are countless additional experiences a counselor may note in a client who has suffered religious abuse. However, noting the common experiences here may help a counselor to reflect back, normalize, and process with the client in order to help them feel heard.

# References

Bailie, G. (2004). *Violence unveiled: Humanity at the crossroads.* New York: Crossroad.

Bottoms, B. L., Goodman, G. S., Tolou-Shams, M., Diviak, K. R., & Shaver, P. R. (2015). Religion-related child maltreatment: A profile of cases encountered by legal and social service agencies. *Behavioral Sciences & The Law, 33,* 561–579. doi: 10.1002/bsl.2192

Celano, M., Hazzard, A., Webb, C., & McCall, C. (1996). Treatment of traumagenic beliefs among sexually abused girls and their mothers: An evaluation study. *Journal of Abnormal Child Psychology, 24*(1), 1–17. doi: 10.1007/BF01448370

Doyle, T. (2003). Roman Catholic clericalism, religious duress, and clergy sex abuse. *Pastoral Psychology, 51,* 189–231.

Doyle, T. P. (2006). Clericalism: Enabler of clergy sexual abuse. *Pastoral Psychology, 54,* 189–213. doi: 10.1007/s11089-006-6323-x

Farrell, D. (2004). An historical viewpoint of sexual abuse perpetrated by clergy and religious. *Journal of Religion & Abuse, 6*(2), 41–80.

Finkelhor, D. (1987). The trauma of child sexual abuse: Two models. *Journal of Interpersonal Violence, 2*(4), 348–366. doi: 10.1177/088626058700200402

Finkelhor, D., & Browne, A. (1985). The traumatic impact of child sexual abuse: A conceptualization. *American Journal of Orthopsychiatry, 55*(4), 530–541. doi: 10.1111/j.1939-0025.1985.tb02703.x

Gavrielides, T. (2012). Clergy child sexual abuse and the restorative justice dialogue. *Journal of Church and State, 55*(4), 617–639. doi: 10.1093/jcs/css041

Hogan, L. (2011). Clerical and religious child abuse: Ireland and beyond. *Theological Studies, 72,* 170–186.

Oakley, L. R., & Kinmond, K. S. (2014). Developing safeguarding policy and practice for spiritual abuse. *The Journal of Adult Protection, 16*(2), 87–95. doi: 10.1108/JAP-07-2013-0033

Pargament, K. I., Murray-Swank, N. A., & Mahoney, A. (2008). Problem and solution: The spiritual dimension of clergy sexual abuse and its impact on survivors. *Journal Of Child Sexual Abuse, 17*(3–4), 397–420.

Redmond, S. A. (1996). God died and nobody gave a funeral. *Pastoral Psychology, 45*(1), 41–47.

Rossetti, S. J. (1995). The impact of child sexual abuse on attitudes toward God and the Catholic church. *Child Abuse & Neglect, 19*(12), 1469–1481.

Swindle, P. J. (2017). *A twisting of the sacred: The lived experience of religious abuse.* The University of North Carolina at Greensboro, ProQuest Dissertations Publishing. 10264116.

# 4 Assessing Religious Abuse

Many psychotherapy organizations and licensure boards recognize the importance of assessing a client's religious or spiritual worldview or background (or lack thereof). The American Counseling Association (ACA) Code of Ethics (2014), the Association for Spiritual, Ethical, and Religious Values in Counseling (ASERVIC) Spiritual Competencies (2009) endorsed by ACA, and the Council for Accreditation of Counseling and Related Educational Programs (CACREP, 2016) all contain directives about the importance of assessing for a client's identification with spirituality and/or religion. In their section on Social and Cultural Diversity, the 2016 CACREP standards require that accredited counseling curriculums address "the impact of spiritual beliefs on clients' and counselors' worldviews" (Section 2.F.2.g, p. 10).

The ACA has an entire division of the organization dedicated to the ethical inclusion of religion and spirituality in counseling called the "Association for Spiritual, Ethical, and Religious Values in Counseling" (ASERVIC). ASERVIC has adopted a set of competencies by which all counselors are expected to abide. These competencies include the expectation that professional counselors have a basic understanding of common beliefs regarding spirituality and religion (Competency 1) and that, as stated in Competency 2, "The professional counselor recognizes that the client's beliefs (or absence of beliefs) about spirituality and/or religion are central to his or her worldview and can influence psychosocial functioning" (Cashwell & Watts, 2010, p. 5).

The ASERVIC Spiritual Competencies also include a description of the importance of assessing early in the counseling relationship. Competency 10 states, "During the intake and assessment processes, the professional counselor strives to understand a client's spiritual and/or religious perspective by gathering information from the client and/or other sources" (Cashwell & Watts, 2010, p. 5).

Although there are many ways that therapists perform an intake and overall assessment of a new client and many different assessment forms for a wide variety of presenting issues, there is a glaring lack of formally validated assessment tools available for assessing religious harm in a client. Koch and Edstrom (2022) have developed the Religious Harm and Abuse Scale and

DOI: 10.4324/9781003029465-5

have made it publically available at https://www.dankochwords.com/spiritual-abuse-screener.html. Koch (2022) reports, "The Spiritual Harm & Abuse Scale (SHAS) is a 27-item self-report inventory capturing both exposure to potentially spiritually abusive experiences in Christian church or group settings and common internal responses to such experiences" and includes questions about lived experiences and emotional reactions. Counselors should keep in mind that experiences of religious abuse or trauma may intertwine with other types of trauma and/or mental health reactions. Therefore, assessments for other trauma-related or mental diagnoses such as post-traumatic stress disorder, major depression, or anxiety disorders would also be appropriate.

Counselors may also choose to assess in a less formal manner as part of the overall counseling process. When assessing as described above for a client's spiritual or religious worldview, counselors should remember the ASERVIC Competency 11, which states that "When making a diagnosis, the professional counselor recognizes that the client's spiritual and/or religious perspectives can a.) enhance well-being; b) contribute to the client problems; and/or c) exacerbate symptoms" (Cashwell & Watts, 2010, p. 5) It is typical for therapists to include basic questions about this aspect of clients' lives on an intake form and when gathering social history information. However, it is important for counselors to assess for both positive (coping, support) and negative impacts of this aspect of a client's identity.

Clients may answer this question with a label or a religious affiliation for their answer, so a therapist will get broader and more meaningful information if they follow up with questions such as "What does your religious identity mean to you?" "How does/did it impact you?" "What role does religion play in your life now?" The therapist should also broach the topic of religious abuse and open the door for a client to share experiences that might not have been supportive or positive for them. This can be as simple as "Did you have any negative or harmful experiences in your religious life?" or may include normalizing experiences of religious abuse by broaching in this way, "It is normal for many people to have experienced their religious system in a harmful way, in a way some might call abusive. I wonder if anything like that happened to you?"

Therapists should keep in mind the wide variety of types of religious abuse. As described in Chapter 2, there are three main categories that most experiences of religious abuse fall under.

The three broad categories of religious abuse described to this point in the scholarly literature are as follows:

1. Abuse perpetrated by religious leadership, typically an individual leader
2. Abuse perpetrated by a religious group, directed either toward an individual or toward a group of people
3. Abuse in which the abuse itself has a religious component to it (Swindle, 2017).

Clients may not understand that religious abuse can happen in many forms, and some clients feel comforted when their therapist names their experiences as abusive or traumatic (Swindle, 2017). As part of the ongoing assessment, therapists may also choose to reflect some of the common experiences described in Chapter 3 such as feelings of betrayal, abuse of the power of the sacred, and emotional trauma, and allow the client to assess if those experiences resonate with theirs. Therapists may also incorporate assessments for a diagnosis of major depression, anxiety, trauma-related disorders, or substance-related disorders, but help the client to understand how experiences of religious abuse may have contributed to or triggered the symptoms of such a diagnosis.

As the understanding of religious abuse evolves, it is expected that more formal assessment tools will emerge. However, whether or not a formal instrument is used to help a client understand their experience, therapists should always be broaching the topic with their clients and providing a space for them to bring issues of religious abuse into the counseling space.

## References

American Counseling Association. (2014). *2014 ACA code of ethics*. Retrieved April 8, 2015, from http://www.counseling.org/docs/ethics/2014-aca-code-of-ethics.pdf

Association for Spiritual, Ethical and Religious Values in Counseling. (2009). *Spiritual competencies: Competencies for addressing spiritual and religious issues in counseling*. Retrieved April 8, 2015, from http://www.aservic.org/wp-content/uploads/2010/04/Spiritual-Competencies-Printer-friendly1.pdf

CACREP. (2016). *2016 CACREP standards*. Retrieved March 7, 2016, from http://www.cacrep.org/wp-content/uploads/2016/02/2016-Standards-with-Glossary-rev-2.2016.pdf

Cashwell, C. S., & Watts, R. E. (2010). The new ASERVIC competencies for addressing spiritual and religious issues in counseling. *Counseling and Values, 55*(1), 2–5.

Koch, D. (2022). *Spiritual abuse screener*. Retrieved January 5, 2023, from https://www.dankochwords.com/spiritual-abuse-screener.html

Koch, D., & Edstrom, L. (2022). Development of the spiritual harm and abuse scale. *Journal for the Scientific Study of Religion, 61*, 476–506. doi: 10.1111/jssr.12792

Swindle, Paula J. (2017). *A twisting of the sacred: The lived experience of religious abuse*. The University of North Carolina at Greensboro, ProQuest Dissertations Publishing. 10264116.

# 5 Characteristics of Healthy and Harmful Religious Systems

In this chapter, we will explore the characteristics of religious systems that may make them more likely to perpetuate and/or tolerate instances of religious abuse. The authors acknowledge that harm, abuse, and trauma can occur in any system, including any religious system. However, there are some dynamics and structures that may make it easier for the abusers to carry out and cloak the abuse. These dynamics include how dialogue is encouraged or discouraged within the system, how much authority is allowed to be questioned, and whether or not a hierarchical structure is in place of the leaders being closer to God than others.

Power and control are a part of any abuse situation. Therefore, any system that intentionally creates a separation of power and concentrates more power at the top of that system is one in which abuse can slip in a bit easier. If a church is structured in such a way that the authority is placed all or mostly at the top in the hands of a few or a single leader, members of that church may feel less comfortable questioning that authority, speaking up when they see possible instances of abuse, or may not even understand that abuse is occurring since they may view the leadership as being all powerful (Doyle, 2006).

A system such as this may discourage questions altogether, undermining the voice of any who dare to speak out or stand up for a victim of religious abuse. If the pervasive theology and doctrine is such that those leaders at the top who hold all of the power and all of the authority are actually closer to God, then anyone who questions this may be seen or punished as someone who is defying or questioning God. Some abusers may actually seek out a position of leadership in the church because of this proximity to power given to them in this role.

Connected to this, a structure where leadership is concentrated at the top is likely to lack transparency. The actions and processes within the system are easier to escape scrutiny if no one is allowed to question those carrying out the processes. For example, instances of financial abuse within a church are easier if there are no policies or procedures for accounting or if there is no financial report provided to church members. Instances of physical or sexual abuse from a minister may be more likely to occur if the victim sees the minister as empowered by God and no one questions time alone with the victim. The victim may also be very aware of the perception of the leader within the system and, knowing the power and control they hold, may be much less likely to report the abuse knowing what an uphill climb they have in being believed by a group of people who have not been allowed to question their abuser in any other situation (Swindle, 2017).

Alternately, healthy religious systems often have very different structures when it comes to power and control. Healthy systems can tolerate and even encourage questions about the theology, the structure, and the processes. Healthy systems have policies and procedures in place to guide the inner workings of the church rather than allowing a single person or few people to control how things work and how decisions are made. Health systems promote transparency as to how decisions are made, and often involve the larger group in the making of those decisions. There may be leaders in place, but everyone has access to those leaders and feels some ownership in the leadership of the system. People are not afraid to ask questions and do not have to feel anxiety about having different opinions or interpretations than the group or the leaders.

An often telling characteristic of whether a system is healthy or not is how it chooses to respond to allegations of abuse. In unhealthy systems, one might see a system "circling the wagons" and looking for ways to undermine the accusations. There may be a tendency to protect the system rather than support the possible victim. The voice raising the concern may be silenced while the system responds with defensiveness.

However, in a healthy system, there is a willingness to engage in self-examination and to seek the truth rather than spin a narrative that protects the system. A healthy system will look for ways to support the accuser while they are investigating the accusation. A healthy system will provide as much transparency as possible in the process.

Ultimately, the issue of control and how it is wielded is key. In an unhealthy system, the power and control will be concentrated at the top, and those with it will attempt to exert a great deal of control over the rest of the system. In a religious system, the power of the sacred is often the tool used to keep others in line, and this may stem from the aforementioned pervasive messaging that the leaders are more sacred, more holy, and closer to God than anyone else. This exertion of control is seen in its most extreme state in systems that meet classifications for religious cults, but they are seen, to a lesser degree, in unhealthy but more mainstream religious systems.

In contrast, healthy religious systems are driven by the need to serve rather than control. Control is not the end goal, as it is in more unhealthy systems. This willingness to give up control is seen in the trickle down of the other characteristics of healthy systems such as more access to leaders, openness to questions, and support of an accuser during an investigation of religious abuse.

The need to control may also extend to a small group or individual attempting to limit others from having any power or control in the system. Unhealthy systems will often be places where some groups such as women, people of color, or members of the LGBTQ+ (Lesbian, Gay, Bisexual,

Transgender, Queer+) community are marginalized. In contrast, a healthy religious system will seek to be a safe place for all people to feel accepted and affirmed in their identities.

Another characteristic of an unhealthy religious system is one of the experiences described in Swindle's (2017) study on religious abuse where participants reported feeling as though the rules were more important than they were. For example, some reported feeling as though the rule that they stay married was more important to the religious leaders and religious system than them being able to escape physical abuse. They described this as a rigid system where the rule mattered more than they did. In a broader sense, systems that are more rigid and interpret people's experiences through the rules rather than the rules through the experiences of a person may be more likely to see instances of rules being used to harm people.

The characteristics that contribute to an unhealthy religious system create environments that make it more likely for all the different types of religious abuse to occur. They provide a haven for abuse done by religious leaders, they often teach theology that can be harmful, and they empower their congregations to embrace and carry out acts of abuse. Some questions people can ask of themselves and the system to help determine if it is a more healthy or unhealthy religious system are as follows:

- What does this church teach about authority?
- Am I allowed to ask questions if I do not understand or if I disagree with something taught by leadership?
- What will happen if I disagree with the pastor or another leader? How will I be treated?
- Am I allowed to be myself in all my identities in this system? Are there parts of myself that I need to hide? What will happen if I reveal all of who I am?
- How transparent are those in leadership?
- Does this church teach that God loves some more than others? What are the criteria for this?

Of course, systems change over time, and abuse can occur in any system, so this is not an exhaustive list of questions or characteristics to guide an assessment of health of a religious system. However, they may be used to help clients engage in reflection about the system they have been a part of and to validate some experiences of abuse.

## References

Doyle, T. P. (2006). Clericalism: Enabler of clergy sexual abuse. *Pastoral Psychology*, *54*, 189–213. doi: 10.1007/s11089-006-6323-x

Swindle, Paula J. (2017). *A twisting of the sacred: The lived experience of religious abuse*. The University of North Carolina at Greensboro, ProQuest Dissertations Publishing. 10264116.

# 6 Common Victim Populations

As you may have realized from the examples given so far, anyone could become a victim of religious abuse. The kinds of abuse that may occur in a religious system vary widely, and there is no one type of person who might find themselves in a therapist's office seeking counseling for experiences of religious abuse. However, there are some populations and identities who are some of the more common recipients of religious abuse, and we will explore some of those in this chapter, including

- Women
- People who identify as queer or members of the LGBTQ+ (Lesbian, Gay, Bisexual, Transgender, Queer+) community
- Children
- Racial/ethnic minorities
- Pastors
- People who are deconstructing or who have left a religious system
- Non-majority beliefs.

Of course, some people may contain multiple or overlapping identities that fall into more than one of these categories and increase their vulnerability.

## Women

Christianity has historically been viewed as a patriarchal religious system, and although many Christian churches no longer identify as patriarchal, women are especially vulnerable to abuse, especially in those that still do. An obvious example of this is religious systems that do not allow women to serve in leadership. Two participants in Swindle's (2017) study on religious abuse reported their experiences serving in Christian ministries as abusive due to the restrictions that were put on them in their areas of service. Both reported being treated as "less than" and having their leadership abilities and rights questioned to the point that they eventually left the ministry. Many religious systems would not allow a woman to be ordained in the role as a minister or

DOI: 10.4324/9781003029465-7

even a deacon or elder in the first place. Women may experience this as a type of abuse, excluding them from opportunities or being actively discouraged or even bullied if they try.

Women who do find systems in which to serve may still experience difficulty and emotional trauma in the role due to being chronically dismissed or minimized. They may be accepted in their church but may not be able to find acceptance in the larger denominational or religious community around them, which can feel isolating and lonely.

However, a woman does not have to see a role in ministry to be vulnerable to abuse. Theologies of "submissive wives" and women not being allowed a voice in church can lead to abuse of many kinds. Many women have felt pressure from (often male) church leaders, their church community, and interpretations of theology to stay in marriages that are physically or sexually abusive (Swindle, 2017). One woman went so far as to believe the church would let her die rather than allow her to leave her marriage, so she left the church (Swindle, 2017).

Religious systems that teach that there is a superior gender may result in the dehumanization of the "lesser" gender (anything other than a man) and may place women in especially vulnerable positions. The use of the sacred to control can become very dangerous when a husband believes his faith gives him the right to treat his wife in any manner he chooses without repercussion. When the concept of the patriarchy and subjugation of women is legitimized by theology and religious leaders, women lose their voice and their rights. These are a few reasons women are especially vulnerable in abusive religious systems.

## LGBTQIA+/Queer Communities

Members of the LGBTQIA+ community often have similar experiences. Beverly Greene (2013) describes the phenomena of how queer identifying people are often treated in the church as a "legitimized inequality" which she describes as something that "gives license to harm." (p. 41). Some Christian churches have a history of focusing on the LGBTQ community particularly as "sinful," which has resulted in experiences of strong marginalization.

Some members of the queer community feel that they cannot remain in this community and remain in a religious community. Sometimes this is because the theology of the religious community overtly says this to them and they are not allowed to participate, and sometimes this message is sent in more subtle ways as they are marginalized or experience harmful preaching. Rodriguez and Ouellette (2000) described four approaches that people may use when facing conflict between their sexual identity and their religious community or identity. They may

1 Reject the religious identity
2 Reject the sexual identity

3 Compartmentalize
4 Integrate the identities.

All these choices except the last one require some diminishing of oneself, which can result in feelings of worthlessness or internalized critiques. There may be an existential crisis as people internalize the homophobia or transphobia believed by their religious system, and they may worry about their own salvation or going to hell as some religious beliefs may have conveyed to them. There is often angst as they go through a deconstruction process and grieve the loss of their community and, sometimes, their own faith.

People in the LGBTQIA+ community may also experience rejection from their family members due to the religious beliefs of the family. They may lose these relationships and, in some cases, they may lose their home. They may feel diminished as they receive the message that the love of their family is not unconditional.

They may also see churches organize and advocate for stripping them of their human rights such as marriage, job protections, and physical safety as some churches involve themselves in laws and governmental decisions about these things. It is one thing to be told that you cannot marry your partner, and then the harm may be amplified further when you are told this is because God wants it this way and is on their side against you.

There is a movement in some churches and some denominations to push for full acceptance and affirmation and celebration of the LGBTQIA+ community, and some members of this community may be able to find safer religious systems. However, there is a sharp divide in religious communities, and there are still many religious places that are not safe for those who identify as queer.

## Children

Children are also more vulnerable to religious abuse. They are already in the place of the least power and control and susceptible to the abuse of others. They are often conditioned to follow the rules and not question authority, and, in cases of religious abuse, that authority is often seen as coming from God. They may see their parents happy in a system that is abusing them, or praising or praying for a religious leader that is harming them, and this makes it even less likely they will report any abuse or be believed if they do report it. Church is also a place that many parents assume to be safe and will not question sending their child there for long periods of time for teaching and service, which can lend itself access for the abuser.

## Racial/Ethnic Minorities

The teachings of the Christian church and biblical theology have also been used to defend and promote racism and the marginalization of racial and ethnic minorities (Greene, 2013). The justification of enslaving other humans was justified by biblical scripture, and the ramification of this continues. The impact may be felt in individual ways such as a pastor refusing to marry an interracial couple or, on a much broader systemic level, as religious institutions refusing to take any ownership for the broader racism to which they have contributed.

## Pastors

Although it might be contradictory, pastors are often victims of religious abuse from the religious systems that employ them. Pastors are often held to impossibly high standards and not allowed to set boundaries around work. Pastors are expected to be available at all times when someone is sick, or in crisis, or when there is an event at the church (even if the pastor is not involved). People are often very passionate about their religion and may have strong feelings about how their church is to be run, which may contradict another member of the congregation with equally strong feelings. Pastors have to navigate these sometimes contradictory expectations, always with the knowledge that the church could decide they should not be their pastor anymore. Some pastors are not given a living wage because the church feels they should see their job as a service. Pastors absorb a lot of the emotions, grief, and trauma of their congregants and may experience secondary trauma themselves. The family members of pastors may become resentful as they watch how much is demanded of the pastor and how they often come last in the list of demands on the pastor's time. So, although pastors do have the power required to be the religious abuser, sometimes that power can flip and pastors can be on the receiving end of religious abuse.

## Deconstructing or Leaving Religious System

People who decide to leave a religious system can also experience religious harm. They may deconstruct their religious beliefs which may be ingrained in them from an early age, and this can be a very painful and confusing process. They may experience rejection from their family as their beliefs no longer align, and there may be a grieving process for their relationships that have changed, for their own belief system, and for the religious community. There may be a trauma bond with that system, making it difficult to leave.

## Non-majority Beliefs

Because we are focusing mainly on religious abuse in the Christian community, there may be those who are in a predominantly Christian area who are unsafe or at least "othered" due to their different beliefs. In the United States, Christians are in the majority and carry the most power, and other religions may experience discrimination. As we see a rise of Christian nationalism, the rights of other religions become even more precarious.

This is not an exhaustive list of the most vulnerable populations for religious abuse, but these are populations who do commonly report experiences of religious abuse. While it can happen to anyone, therapists should pay particular attention to the possibility of abuse in the groups described here, as well as how the intersection of multiple vulnerable identities can amplify the experience of abuse.

## References

Greene, B. (2013). The use and abuse of religious beliefs in dividing and conquering between socially marginalized groups: The same-sex marriage debate. *Psychology of Sexual Orientation and Gender Diversity, 1*, 35–44.

Rodriguez, E. M., & Ouellette, S. C. (2000). Gay and lesbian Christians: Homosexual and religious identity integration in the members and participants of a gay-positive church. *Journal for the Scientific Study of Religion, 39*(3), 333–347. doi: 10.1111/0021-8294.00028

Swindle, P. J. (2017). *A twisting of the sacred: The lived experience of religious abuse*. The University of North Carolina at Greensboro, ProQuest Dissertations Publishing. 10264116.

# Section II
# Ethics

# 7 Ethical Principles in the Treatment of Religious Abuse

It is imperative that therapists thoughtfully consider ethics in treating individuals who have experienced religious abuse. The research on ethics abounds (including principle and virtue ethics) and ethical codes varies across mental health disciplines. In Chapter 8, we will (1) outline the basic tenets of principle and virtue ethics; (2) discuss the ethical codes that apply to religious abuse within the context of psychology, social work, and counseling; and (3) present and analyze a case of religious abuse. In Chapter 8, we will continue this discussion by outlining a step-by-step analysis of religious abuse through an ethical decision-making model.

## Principle and Virtue Ethics

Before diving into the types of ethics and discipline-specific ethical codes, it is important to examine what is meant by the term ethics. According to Remley and Herlihy (2001), "Ethics is a discipline within philosophy that is concerned with human conduct and moral decision making" (Remley & Herlihy, 2001, p. 2). Morals are similar to ethics; however, they are more often nested within an individual's cultural values. Laws are also somewhat similar to ethics; however, laws constitute the minimum required level of behavioral compliance, whereas ethics are more aspirational. (In other words, not following a law can land a person in jail; not following an ethical code can lead to professional disciplinary action.) Thus, when we examine the ethical principles of treating religious abuse, we are really presenting the best practices of therapy.

As discussed in earlier chapters, religious abuse is an insidious issue and needs to be treated with the utmost of care and integrity. Essentially, people who are entering therapy with religious abuse are entering from a place of distrust and betrayal (Cashwell & Swindle, 2018). The framework of religion, which is often designed as a moral guide for love and goodness, has been shattered, and thus, it is critical that therapists abide by the highest ethical standards in treatment. One foundational element in ethical practice is consideration of and adherence to principle ethics.

DOI: 10.4324/9781003029465-9

## Principle Ethics

"Principles are more general and fundamental than moral rules or codes and serve as their foundation" (Kitchener, 1984, p. 46). According to Kitchener's (1984) foundational article on principle ethics, therapists should follow their ethical codes up until they become too ambiguous or contradictory. This ambiguous and contradictory nature is certainly likely, as some therapists, such as counselors, often are obligated to adhere to multiple codes of ethics (e.g., ACA Code of Ethics, 2014; NBCC Code of Ethics, 2016). It is during these times that principle ethics become guidelines for reasoned behavior.

Kitchener (1984) first outlined five major principle ethics: autonomy, nonmaleficence, beneficence, justice, and fidelity. *Autonomy* includes two concepts: "freedom of action" and "freedom of choice" (Kitchener, 1984, p. 46). In the context of religious abuse, autonomy could be the act of allowing the client freedom in their religious decisions. Because clients who have struggled with religious abuse often feel a sense of powerlessness (Cashwell & Swindle, 2018), it is critical that therapists honor their autonomy. For example, a client may present a clear case where a pastor is coercing her to donate money that she doesn't have to the church. A therapist honoring autonomy may explore this issue and the client's feelings associated with it but, ultimately, empower the client to decide what to choose and how to act.

*Nonmaleficence* is the principle ethic of "do no harm" (Kitchener, 1984, p. 47). Stemming from the medical field, nonmaleficence is ultimately concerned with preserving the well-being of the patient or client. Within a case of religious abuse, nonmaleficence could be characterized by the therapist's care not to recapitulate a harmful power imbalance similar to the client's experience in a religious context. Furthermore, doing no harm could be a therapist ensuring that clients' religious concerns are validated and processed, rather than cast aside or dismissed.

*Beneficence* is the flip side of nonmaleficence and is concerned with "doing good" and promoting "positive growth" (Kitchener, 1984, p. 49). In other words, it is important that therapists and helping professionals seek to do just that – *help*. In a case of religious abuse, this may be the practice of preserving the client's healthy religious and spiritual beliefs while processing the harmful experiences the client has endured.

In its most basic sense, *justice* is the practice of being fair (Kitchener, 1984). Although this ethical principle sounds simple, practicing justice in therapy can be difficult. For example, if two clients enter therapy, one who earns a six-figure salary a year and one who earns minimum wage, does justice mean that the therapist charges them the same amount for services? These types of scenarios certainly complicate the application of fair practice. Furthermore, justice is not only concerned with the treatment of individual clients, but also the fair treatment of groups and members of society. In the case of religious abuse, a therapist may have to question fair treatment in working with a client experiencing Christian religious abuse (as a majority religion in the United States) versus a client experiencing Muslim religious abuse (as a minority religion in the United States). In these cases, and as will be discussed later, therapists' self-awareness becomes paramount.

Finally, *fidelity* is the practice of "promise keeping" or "loyalty" (Kitchener, 1984, p. 51). A therapist who is practicing fidelity follows through on agreed-upon plans, keeps their promises, and acts with integrity. Therapists and clients often agree upon these conditions during the first meeting when signing the informed consent form. In cases of religious abuse where clients may have already been betrayed by a person in power and feel suspicious of the therapist, it is even more important that therapists act with great integrity. In essence, they are helping the client reestablish trust in the world not only through explicit therapeutic endeavors but also through implicit ways of being.

In addition to autonomy, nonmaleficence, beneficence, justice, and fidelity, *veracity* is sometimes included within the ethical principles. According to Remley and Herlihy (2001), "veracity means truthfulness" (p. 7). In this regard, therapists strive for honesty within the therapeutic encounter. In practice with clients struggling with religious abuse, this might include being honest and straightforward about the definition of abuse and its insidious forms of manifestation.

Taken together, the ethical principles undergird moral decision-making, especially where discipline-specific ethical codes may prove confusing and/or contradictory. However, scholars such as Jordan and Meara (1990) have illuminated the limitations of principle ethics and have proposed *virtue ethics* as another important component of ethical practice.

### Virtue Ethics

According to Jordan and Meara (1990), ethical principles answer the question "What shall I do?" whereas virtue ethics answer the question "Who shall I be?" (p. 107). Rather than assuming that ethical decision-making is done in a personal, dispassionate, and detached void, Jordan and Meara (1990) emphasize the personal characteristics of the therapist guide decision-making, such as *prudence, discretion, perseverance, courage, integrity, humility,* and *hope* (list on p. 110). Other virtues may include *acceptance of emotion, self-awareness,* and *interdependence with the community* (Remley & Herlihy, 2001, p. 8). Within the context of virtue ethics, the most important consideration is the training – and perhaps gatekeeping – of the therapist's character.

We consider virtue ethics a critical area of exploration within the context of religious abuse. Virtues and character education are often relegated to the religious realm of children's upbringing. In other words, it is often within religious settings and religious stories where students learn about prudence, discretion, courage, humility, and hope. For example, within the Christian tradition, children may learn about courage after reading the story of David and Goliath, or they may learn about perseverance after hearing more about the Apostle Paul's faith journey. After having experienced religious abuse, clients may feel betrayed not only by their religious institution but also by the virtues taught – and perhaps hypocritically not followed – within the religious institution. It becomes even more important, then, that therapists embody these virtue ethics and aspire to be a person of true integrity.

## Discipline-Specific Ethical Codes

Psychology, social work, and counseling are three major helping professions grounded in the practice of ethical behaviors. From the beginning of their educational and training programs in these areas, therapists-in-training are immersed in the consistent and pervasive practice of analyzing and applying ethical codes. Although it is beyond the scope of this book to review the ethical codes within each discipline, we examine the codes within each discipline that apply specifically to the treatment of religious abuse.

One could argue that there are more similarities than differences across the specific codes of ethics written for psychologists, social workers, and counselors. At the time of this writing, psychologists adhere to the *Ethical Principles of Psychologists and Code of Conduct* (American Psychological Association [APA], 2017); social workers abide by the *Code of Ethics of the National Association of Social Workers* (National Association of Social Workers [NASW], 2017); and counselors ascribe to the *ACA Code of Ethics* (American Counseling Association [ACA], 2014). Across each discipline's ethical codes, the three areas such as respect, nondiscrimination, and competence contain many of the specific codes related to ethical treatment of religious abuse.

### *Respect*

Respect is often one of the first areas within each discipline's respective codes of ethics. Grounded in the ethical principles of autonomy, nonmaleficence, and beneficence, respect centers on honoring and regarding the humanity of another person. This becomes especially critical for therapists working within the realm of religious abuse, as clients have often felt betrayed by their religious leaders and community members (Cashwell & Swindle, 2018).

In psychology, one of the first overarching ethical principles for psychologists is *Principle E: Respect for People's Rights and Dignity*, which states

> Psychologists are aware of and respect cultural, individual, and role differences, including those based on age, gender, gender identity, race, ethnicity, culture, national origin, religion, sexual orientation, disability, language, and socioeconomic status, and consider these factors when working with members of such groups. Psychologists try to eliminate the effect on their work of biases based on those factors, and they do not

knowingly participate in or condone activities of others based upon such prejudices.

(APA, 2017, p. 4)

In this regard, psychologists are expected to develop awareness of their prejudices and biases and respect cultural differences within the therapeutic relationship. With respect to religious abuse, psychologists are aware of their own biases surrounding religious and spiritual beliefs and ensure these do not impact ethical treatment.

The prominence of respect is evident in social workers' codes of ethics as well. According to the National Association for Social Workers (2017),

> Social workers respect and promote the right of clients to self-determination and assist clients in their efforts to identify and clarify their goals. Social workers may limit clients' right to self-determination when, in the social workers' professional judgment, clients' actions or potential actions pose a serious, foreseeable, and imminent risk to themselves or others.
>
> (1.02)

This ethical code highlights the ways that basic respect is woven into the principle of client autonomy – or self-determination – for social workers. Clients who have survived religious abuse may not have had the experience of personal autonomy based on respect, and thus, they may struggle to develop their own identity and beliefs free from the control of others.

Counselors are also held to an ethical principle based on respect:

> Counselors are aware of—and avoid imposing—their own values, attitudes, beliefs, and behaviors. Counselors respect the diversity of clients, trainees, and research participants and seek training in areas in which they are at risk of imposing their values onto clients, especially when the counselor's values are inconsistent with the client's goals or are discriminatory in nature.
>
> (ACA, 2014, A.4.b)

Within this ethical principle, counselors are encouraged to develop awareness around their own biases, which can certainly impact the treatment of religious abuse. For example, if a counselor does not respect religion, in general, they are unlikely to treat cases of religious abuse sensitively. Similarly, if a counselor is highly religious, they may also struggle to treat cases of religious abuse prudently. Taken together, each discipline's code of ethics underscores a basic tenet of respecting clients, which is critical in the treatment of religious abuse.

## *Nondiscrimination*

Nondiscrimination is another common ethical area within each discipline's codes of ethics. The practice of nondiscrimination is rooted in the ethical principles of nonmaleficence, beneficent, and justice, and it is critical when considering cases of religious abuse. Because discrimination is more likely within areas of difference (such as religious difference between the counselor and the client), it is especially important to abide by nondiscrimination codes.

Within the code of ethics for psychologists,

> In their work-related activities, psychologists do not engage in unfair discrimination based on age, gender, gender identity, race, ethnicity, culture, national origin, religion, sexual orientation, disability, socioeconomic status, or any basis proscribed by law.
>
> (APA, 2007, 3.01)

As the reader can see, religion is listed as a construct to consider when practicing nondiscrimination. In other words, psychologists need to be aware of their own religious and spiritual beliefs to ensure that they don't influence their therapy with clients – especially clients where religious abuse is a major concern.

Social workers are also held to a high standard of nondiscrimination, as evidenced in the following three ethical codes:

> Social workers should have a knowledge base of their clients' cultures and be able to demonstrate competence in the provision of services that are sensitive to clients' cultures and to differences among people and cultural groups.
>
> (NASW, 2017, 1.05b)

> Social workers should obtain education about and seek to understand the nature of social diversity and oppression with respect to race, ethnicity, national origin, color, sex, sexual orientation, gender identity or expression, age, marital status, political belief, religion, immigration status, and mental or physical ability.
>
> (NASW, 2017, 1.05c)

> Social workers should not practice, condone, facilitate, or collaborate with any form of discrimination on the basis of race, ethnicity, national origin, color, sex, sexual orientation, gender identity or expression, age, marital status, political belief, religion, immigration status, or mental or physical ability.
>
> (NASW, 2017, 4.02)

Within these codes of ethics, it is clear that social workers should be knowledgeable about other cultures, should seek additional education when faced with a lack of knowledge, and should actively aspire toward nondiscrimination. When considering religious abuse, it is important that social workers obtain the appropriate information and education in order to treat clients in a trauma-informed, nondiscriminatory manner. Without this knowledge and awareness of the insidious ways that personal religious beliefs can impact therapy, therapists could certainly do harm to their clients.

In addition to psychologists and social workers, counselors are held to a standard of nondiscrimination:

> Counselors do not condone or engage in discrimination against prospective or current clients, students, employees, supervisees, or research participants based on age, culture, disability, ethnicity, race, religion/spirituality, gender, gender identity, sexual orientation, marital/ partnership status, language preference, socioeconomic status, immigration status, or any basis proscribed by law.
>
> (ACA, 2014, C.5)

Again, religion and spirituality are noted as specific areas of consideration within this ethical code of nondiscrimination. It is interesting to note that counselors' codes of ethics apply not just to clients but also to students, supervisees, etc. Thus, nondiscrimination is not just bound within the therapeutic relationship but also expected within all professional relationships.

Taken together, it is clear that nondiscrimination is an important ethical code traversing each discipline's codes of ethics. Furthermore, in all three of these examples, religion is specifically named as an important consideration.

## *Competence*

In addition to respect and nondiscrimination, competence is an important ethical code occurring across each discipline's codes of ethics. Furthermore, competence is critical in the treatment of religious abuse, as it is important that therapists be knowledgeable about the benefits and possible drawbacks of religion, understand the therapeutic power differential as a possible trigger for clients who have experienced religious abuse, be familiar with trauma-informed therapy, and, probably most importantly, ensure not to recapitulate any aspects of the abuse.

Psychologists are expected to demonstrate competence in working with various populations. In the second section on competence, their ethical codes state

> Where scientific or professional knowledge in the discipline of psychology establishes that an understanding of factors associated with age, gender, gender identity, race, ethnicity, cultural, national origin, religion, sexual orientation, disability, language, or socioeconomic status is essential for effective implementation of their services or research, psychologists have or obtain the training, experience, consultation, or supervision necessary

to ensure the competence of their services, or they make appropriate referrals.

(APA, 2017, 2.01)

In this code, psychologists not only highlight the imperative nature of competence within psychology but also specifically include religion as an area of needed competence.

Social workers are held to a similar standard:

> Social workers should provide services and represent themselves as competent only within the boundaries of their education, training, license, certification, consultation received, supervised experience, or other relevant professional experience.
>
> (NASW, 2017, 1.04a)

> Social workers should provide services in substantive areas or use intervention techniques or approaches that are new to them only after engaging in appropriate study, training, consultation, and supervision from people who are competent in those interventions or techniques.
>
> (NASW, 2017, 1.04b)

Within both of these codes, it is clear that social workers should be aware of and practice only within the bounds of their competence and ensure that they seek training in areas where they are lacking. Reading this book and consulting with experts in religious abuse is a great way to increase competence in the area of religious abuse.

Finally, counselors are also held to a high standard of competence:

> Counselors practice only within the boundaries of their competence, based on their education, training, supervised experience, state and national professional credentials, and appropriate professional experience. Whereas multicultural counseling competency is required across all counseling specialties, counselors gain knowledge, personal awareness, sensitivity, dispositions, and skills pertinent to being a culturally competent counselor in working with a diverse client population.
>
> (ACA, 2014, C.2.a)

> Counselors recognize that support networks hold various meanings in the lives of clients and consider enlisting the support, understanding, and involvement of others (e.g., religious/ spiritual/community leaders, family members, friends) as positive resources, when appropriate, with client consent.
>
> (ACA, 2014, A.1.d)

## Ethical Principles in Treatment of Religious Abuse 59

This second ethical code is interesting in that counselors are expected to recognize the importance of support networks in clients' lives and draw upon them when necessary and appropriate. In the case of religious abuse, for example, a competent counselor might have a referral list of religious figures who could support a client's healing process (rather than retraumatizing them).

In summary, it is important that therapists who work with cases of religious abuse be highly respectful, nondiscriminatory, and competent. These basic ethical tenets underscore the integrity of the therapist and ensure that the client receives appropriate care. In the following section, we outline a case study applying many of these ethical principles and codes.

## Case Study

### *First Session*

Jaime is a 23-year-old Mexican American male who has entered therapy due to feelings of depression and anxiety. His counselor, Maria, a 40-year-old Latinx woman, begins the first session by exploring his current and past feelings of anxiety and depression. About halfway into the first session, Jaime reports that he was a devout Catholic and used to attend Mass twice a week. He then looks away, eyes downcast, and softly reports that he left the church six months ago. Maria promptly notices his change in tone and pace, and begins to explore further: "Jaime, I noticed that your voice became softer and you looked away as you talked about leaving the church."

"Yeah," Jaime replies, "I wasn't welcome there anymore…"

"You weren't welcome?" Maria softly inquires.

"Yeah, well, um…" Jaime trips over his words, clearly struggling to tell his story. "I guess, I don't know… I just wasn't welcome because of who I am."

Not wanting to push him too hard, Maria simply paraphrases, "So there was something about who you are that led to this feeling of not being welcomed…?"

"Yeah, um, well…" Jaime takes a deep breath, "About six months ago, I told the priest that… well, that I had some feelings toward one of my friends…" He looks aside, waiting for Maria to pick up on the story so he doesn't have to finish.

"Ah – so you were maybe feeling attracted to another man, and you were struggling with it, so you told your priest – looking for help – and somehow it left you feeling like you weren't welcome anymore."

At this reflection, Jaime becomes visibly angry:

> It didn't *somehow* leave me feeling that way! They told me that! The priest said that it was against God's will in the Bible – that I was going to hell! He told others – everyone else in the whole place. It was like he shouted it

from the rooftop and the whole community turned on me. I can't help with the youth group, I can't volunteer with the luncheons, I'm like a heathen!

Maria validates his anger, "I can see how angry this has made you. Feels like your whole community turned on you."

Jaime's eyes fill with tears and he looks away, "They turned on me."

At this point, it is important to stop and examine Jaime's situation a little more closely. An astute therapist would begin to ascertain that Jaime has experienced religious abuse, encompassing all three of Swindle's (2017) categories: abuse by a religious leader, abuse by a religious community, and abuse with a religious element. As we understand the situation up until this point, Jaime's priest turned on him when Jaime expressed feelings of same-sex attraction. Because the priest also told other community members, who then turned on Jaime, he meets the qualification for abuse by a religious community. Finally, Jaime's priest and community members told him that according to the Bible, he was condemned to hell for his same-sex attraction, which constitutes abuse with a religious component. With this knowledge, Maria begins to carefully consider ethical principles, ethical virtues, and discipline-specific ethical codes as she adopts a trauma-informed approach to treating the religious abuse while also honoring and affirming his emerging identity.

## Second Session

In the second session, Maria opens the session by continuing to explore and assess Jaime's experience, emotions, thoughts, and reactions.

> Jaime, I'm aware that last week was a really difficult session. You started by talking a little more about your anxiety and depression, and close to the end of the session, you disclosed more about why you left your church. I'm aware that there are lots of places where we could focus today, and I also want to make sure to provide you with the space to process what you feel like is most important. (Note emphasis on ethical principle of autonomy.)

"Yeah, it actually felt good to get some of that off my chest last week…, but then when I left, it was like it all came flooding back," Jaime describes.

Maria softly follows, "Everything came flooding back."

> Yeah, it was like I was there again. I was exposed for the sinful, dirty person that I am – in front of all those people – in front of my friends, my priest, the church leaders. They were all scorning me – like chastising me and banishing me to hell.

At the end of this statement, Jaime gazes off blankly into space, frozen. Understanding the indications of trauma, Maria begins to adopt a trauma-informed lens to further conceptualize and treat his experience of religious abuse.

"Jaime, I'm hearing that this was a traumatic experience for you," Maria reflects.

Utilizing a trauma-informed lens (see Cashwell & Swindle, 2018; Swindle, 2017) is critical when working with survivors of religious abuse. In fact, one of the first tasks of the therapist is to help the client own the experience as traumatizing, where appropriate (Cashwell & Swindle, 2018). Utilizing evidence-based trauma-informed interventions underscore the competency of the therapist, which is common across discipline-specific ethical codes. Furthermore, using trauma-informed interventions with the client also highlights the ethical principles of beneficence (doing good) and nonmaleficence (do no harm). In Chapter 8, we will further discuss the tenets of a trauma-informed approach, including the six guiding principles of trauma-informed care (CDC, 2020).

### Third Session

"Jaime," Maria starts at the beginning of their third session,

> I realize that we have talked quite a bit about your experiences with the church and how traumatic that has been for you, but I'm not sure if we've talked deeper about what your faith means to you as well as what your emerging sexual/affectional orientation means to you. I wonder if we might want to leave space to explore these today…? (Note ethical principle of autonomy here.)
>
> My faith meant everything to me. I grew up Catholic and considered myself a true follower of God. I went to church every week, I volunteered for everything, all of my connections were with people from my church. Well, except for Jace. He's the guy I'm in a relationship with now. I don't consider myself religious now. I can't be gay and be religious.

It is important to note, here, how ethically attuned Maria needs to be in working with Jaime's feelings about his religion and about his sexual/affectional identity. The ethical principle of justice, along with the discipline-specific ethical codes surrounding respect, nondiscrimination, and competence, is critical here. Jaime, who has identified as a gay man, is a member of a minoritized – and often oppressed – population. Furthermore, not ascribing to Christian beliefs further minoritizes him. Maria needs to promote social justice in empowering Jaime, while, at the same time, she needs to be incredibly competent and aware of her own preconceived assumptions and biases around religion and sexual/affectional orientation.

For example, imagine that Maria is a devout Catholic who internally agrees with the church leaders' judgment about Jaime. Similarly, what if Maria has never been religiously affiliated and believes that all religions, at their core, are divisive and judgmental. Her own beliefs could impact her work with Jaime if she is not highly self-aware and reflective.

Furthermore, as every client is comprised of multiple intersectional identities, Jaime's emergent identity as a gay man may also trigger certain reactions in Maria. She may harbor some implicit bias around Jaime's sexual/affectional orientation and feel uncomfortable discussing this aspect of his identity in a non-pathologizing manner. On the other hand, she could identify as a queer woman and feel compelled to push Jaime to be out and proud.

The juxtaposition – or intersectionality – of these two aspects of Jaime's identity is an even greater consideration, as it underscores his shifting social location and emerging dissonance. Notice that Jaime has an internal belief that he cannot be both Catholic *and* gay. (And although these two may be salient aspects of Jaime's identity, he may also want to explore his racial background as a Mexican American, his gender identity, etc.) Maria must honor Jaime's autonomy, validate his concerns, and support his movement toward greater healing – based on Jaime's conceptualization of what healing might look like.

Clearly, throughout this case study, we have not "treated" or fully explored Jaime's situation. However, the goal of this case study was to underscore the ethical elements of religious abuse. In our later chapters, we will further delineate trauma-informed treatment interventions for individuals who have experienced religious abuse.

## Conclusion

Religious abuse is often an insidious and traumatic experience for clients, and thus, it is critical that therapists uphold the highest standards of care when treating individuals who have been harmed. This integrity is founded in the ethical principles, virtue ethics, and discipline-specific ethical codes of psychologists, social workers, and counselors. In Chapter 8, we will explore ethical situations in much more detail as we walk through a guiding ethical decision-making model for treatment of religious abuse.

## References

American Counseling Association. (2014). *ACA code of ethics*. Alexandria, VA: Author.
American Psychological Association. (2017). *Ethical principles of psychologists and code of conduct*. Washington, DC: Author.
Cashwell, C. S., & Swindle, P. S. (2018). When religion hurts: Supervising cases of religious abuse. *The Clinical Supervisor, 37*(1), 182–203. doi: 10.1080/07325223.2018.1443305

Centers for Disease Control and Prevention (CDC). (2020). *Infographic: 6 guiding principles to a trauma-informed approach.* Retrieved from https://www.cdc.gov/cpr/infographics/6_principles_trauma_info.htm

Jordan, A. E., & Meara, N. M. (1990). Ethics and the professional practice of psychologists: The role of virtues and principles. *Professional Psychology: Research and Practice, 21*(2), 107–114. https://doi-org.ezproxy.lib.ndsu.nodak.edu/10.1037/0735-7028.21.2.107

Kitchener, K. S. (1984). Intuition, critical evaluation and ethical principles: The foundation for ethical decisions in counseling psychology. *The Counseling Psychologist, 12*(3–4), 43–55. https://doi-org.ezproxy.lib.ndsu.nodak.edu/10.1177/0011000084123005

Kitchener, K. S. (1996). There is more to ethics than principles. *The Counseling Psychologist, 24*(1), 92–97. https://doi-org.ezproxy.lib.ndsu.nodak.edu/10.1177/0011000096241005

National Association of Social Workers. (approved 1996, revised 2017). *Code of ethics of the national association of social workers.* Retrieved from https://www.socialworkers.org/About/Ethics/Code-of-Ethics/Code-of-Ethics-English

National Board for Certified Counselors, Inc., and Affiliates. (2016). *National board for certified counselors code of ethics.* https://www.nbcc.org/Assets/Ethics/NBCC-CodeofEthics.pdf

Remley, Jr., T. P., & Herlihy, B. (2001). *Ethical, legal, and professional issues in counseling.* Upper Saddle River, NJ: Merrill Prentice Hall.

Swindle, Paula J. (2017). *A twisting of the sacred: The lived experience of religious abuse.* The University of North Carolina at Greensboro, ProQuest Dissertations Publishing. 10264116.

# 8 Application of Ethics in Treating Religious Abuse

There are a number of ethical decision-making models across the helping professions; however, we have adopted Forester-Miller and Davis's (2016) oft-used *Practitioner's Guide to Ethical Decision Making*. The model begins with an overview of the foundational principles (autonomy, beneficence, nonmaleficence, justice, and fidelity) of ethical practice discussed in Chapter 7. From there, Forester-Miller and Davis (2016) outline a seven-step model of ethical decision-making (informed by the works of Forester-Miller and Rubenstein [1992], Haas and Malouf [1989], Kitchener [1984], Stadler [1986], and Van Hoose and Paradise [1979]). The seven steps of the model include (1) "identify the problem"; (2) "apply the *ACA Code of Ethics*" (or perhaps another disciplinary code of ethics, as described in Chapter 7); (3) "determine the nature and dimensions of the dilemma"; (4) "generate potential courses of action"; (5) "consider the potential consequences of all options and determine a course of action"; (6) "evaluate the selected course of action"; and (7) "implement the course of action" (Forester-Miller & Davis, 2016, p. 5). Using the following case study, we walk through a description and application of each step of the model.

## Case Study

Natalia is a 34-year-old multiracial woman who emigrated from India with her parents when she was three years old. When she arrived in the United States, her parents joined a Christian nondenominational church, and throughout her life, she has considered the church her second home. When she was 24, she met a white man named Chad and quickly fell in love. They married in Natalia's home church, and Chad became a member as well.

In the beginning, Chad and Natalia seemed the idyllic couple – happy, compatible, social, and hospitable. In fact, they often led church small groups in their home once a week. After a few years, though, Chad lost his job as a construction worker and began drinking alcohol in increasing amounts. Due to the loss in income, he rigidly controlled the finances and required Natalia to give him her waitressing checks and tips and consult with him before she purchased anything.

DOI: 10.4324/9781003029465-10

One night after they had been married for five years, Natalia came home to find Chad inebriated and fuming. He had opened the mail and found a thank-you card from the church for an apparent donation that he had not authorized. Natalia could tell from the moment she entered the home that something was terribly wrong. Chad began shouting and swearing at her, calling her a "bitch" and an "alien whore." She tried to explain that she had only donated a few dollars to support the church's building fund, but he would not listen. The fight escalated until he slapped her across the cheek and pushed her up against the wall. Natalia was devastated, as this had never happened before; she had always considered Chad to be a gentle soul. The next day after he had become more sober, he apologized for his behavior. She decided that, like a good Christian, she would turn the other cheek and forgive him.

For about a week, things seemed to go back to normal, until it happened again. This time, Chad became angry after Natalia forgot to empty the dishwasher. He verbally berated her, insulting her culture and her womanhood. Though he did not strike her, the verbal abuse hurt just as much. And this time, he did not apologize.

Six months passed by with these experiences occurring frequently – mostly after Chad had been drinking heavily, which was now a daily occurrence. Natalia began to feel desperate. She kept the abuse to herself, fearing that if she told anyone, they would also blame her. She sought refuge in waitressing and going to church – times when she was away from Chad. Chad gradually stopped attending church, and church members became concerned and asked her about him. She fabricated a story that he had secured a job that required Sunday morning hours.

About a year after the abuse started, Chad became very angry one Saturday evening and punched Natalia in the face, leaving a large bruise on her cheekbone the next morning. Although she tried to cover it with makeup, church members noticed it immediately and inquired. She told them that she accidentally opened the cupboard door corner on her cheek. Halfway through the service, though, Natalia's heart began racing and she began breathing heavily. Terrified, she thought she might be having a heart attack. Those sitting around her noticed and a kind gentleman walked her out of the service to a bench where she could lay her head down. He cared for her gently until the service was over, and then he encouraged her to go speak with Pastor Josiah. By then, Natalia was so afraid that she agreed and went to talk to the pastor.

Concerned by Natalia's bruised cheek and anxious demeanor, Pastor Josiah agreed to meet with her immediately. It didn't talk long for the whole story to emerge. Through choked sobs and broken sentences, Natalia told the pastor about Chad, his unemployment, his increased drinking, and the abuse. Through it all, Pastor Josiah listened patiently, offering expressions of concern and compassion.

As she finished talking, she continued to cry quietly, the tears silently falling down her cheeks. Depleted by all of the emotion, she sat back, took a deep breath, and waited for Pastor Josiah's response. Mirroring her, he took a deep breath and told her, "Natalia, this is an awful experience that you are facing, and I'm so sorry that you've been struggling." Then he hesitated,

> At the same time, Natalia, it is important that wives submit to their husbands and obey them, as written in Ephesians 5:22. You made a commitment to Chad in your vows – vows that I presided over – and it is important that you pray and work to become a more obedient wife.

Natalia sucked in her breath, feeling the piercing weight of Pastor Josiah's words. She wiped her eyes, smoothed her blouse, and quickly – too quickly – nodded her head.

> I know it might be hard to hear, Natalia, but you made a vow and you need to ensure that you submit to his authority. With your loving devotion, I'm sure that you will be blessed and he will be kind to you. I will pray for you and Chad. And remember, God loves you always.

Natalia walked out of the church that morning a shell of herself – empty, numb, and hopeless. She returned home to a drunken Chad, who was infuriated with her for coming home late from church and not leaving him some lunch to eat. She quietly walked into the kitchen and began making lunch.

A week later, a colleague from her work brought her into the emergency room after she, again, thought she was having a heart attack. The physicians checked her over, determined she was not having a heart attack, and immediately referred her to a clinical mental health counselor named Anya. Anya, a 50-year-old Black woman, had been counseling others – especially those in domestic abuse situations – for 15 years. When Natalia arrived, Anya readily picked up on signs of an abuse survivor, such as the bruises on Natalia's wrists, her confusion about what was happening, her self-blame, and her vacillating loyalty to her husband. At first, Anya sought to simply establish a strong therapeutic alliance with Natalia and ensure her safety. She patiently listened to her story, validated her feelings of hurt and confusion, developed a safety plan, and offered psychoeducational resources and additional community support. Natalia was hesitant to accept the support, believing that she was to blame for the abuse. However, she agreed to move out of the house and into a domestic abuse shelter where she could begin to heal. It was not until the fourth session that Anya realized that there was much more to the story.

"Natalia," Anya started the fourth session,

> I know that we have been talking quite a bit about what you've been experiencing for the past year, and you've accepted some of help from the community... but at the same time, you are really reluctant to entertain the idea that it might not be all your fault.

"It *is* my fault," Natalia asserted with a firm demeanor (which was rare for her).

Anya leaned in, "I could be wrong, but it almost seems as though those words aren't yours... almost as if you heard them from someone else...?"

Natalia quickly looked down and off to the side, becoming quiet and still. After a brief pause, she again asserted, "No, it is. If I were just a better wife..."

"A better wife?" Anya inquired.

"Yeah, like... submitted to him like I should," Natalia explained.

"There's a rule somewhere... you needed to submit to him..." Anya reflected.

Natalia became very quiet and stared at the ground. She rubbed her fingers together.

Anya tried again gently, "Natalia, who said that you needed to submit to him?"

At this question, Natalia winced and turned her head away as a tear fell down her cheek. She quickly wiped it away.

"It's okay if now is not the right time, Natalia. It's okay..."

"Pastor Josiah," Natalia blurted his name out and the tears began to fall faster. She dropped her face into her hands and began sobbing, deep heavy expressions of pain.

"Oh," Anya whispered. "This is so much deeper for you."

"Yeah," Natalia choked through sobs, "He told me," she sniffed, "He told me that I needed to be better... that I needed to submit... that it was in the Bible. I can't... I just don't..." she drifted off and began crying again. "I just have to be a better wife."

At this point, it was clear to Anya that there was much more to the story, and she was also faced with an ethical dilemma. Though she felt fairly clear that Natalia had faced religious abuse, she also knew that Natalia's faith was important to her, and that she truly believed the abuse from her husband was her fault. Anya decided to consult Forester-Miller and Davis's (2016) *Practitioner's Guide to Ethical Decision Making* model.

### *Identify the Problem*

According to Forester-Miller and Davis (2016), the first step in the model is to identify the problem. As one might imagine, this entails fully exploring all aspects of the problem: what type of problem it is, how the practitioner is personally affected, who else is involved, and what type of policies might apply.

In this case, Anya is struggling with how to help Natalia with the apparent religious abuse. In fact, when she lays out the problem, she feels as though, in some ways, Anya needs to focus on the religious abuse and Natalia's associated beliefs before even working on the domestic abuse. In other words, the beliefs that Natalia holds where she should be a "better wife" who "submits to her husband" are so strong for Natalia that it is hard for her to even entertain the notion that she might be stuck in an abusive relationship. However, Anya does not want to invalidate Natalia's beliefs, as she knows that religion is a critical part of Natalia's life.

Another aspect of the problem that Anya is reluctant to explore is her own relationship with religion. Anya was raised Catholic and left the church at 19 after meeting and falling in love with a woman. Since she knew that the church would not condone her choice to engage in a relationship with another female, she decided to leave the church all together. In order to defend against any criticism at the time, she became guarded and angry around religion. She developed a new identity as a humanist and rejected all forms of organized religion, deeming people who followed them ignorant and dualistic. Since then, Anya's acerbic opinions have softened; however, she still does not belong to nor have any interest in organized religion.

As an ethical counselor, Anya knows the importance that spirituality and religion play in peoples' lives, and thus, she tries to respect and honor her clients' perspectives. However, if she is honest with herself, she was really angered by Natalia's story and had the impulse to tell her to leave the church all together – as she herself had done years before. Anya even considered referring her to another counselor who might be more accepting and tolerant of religious viewpoints.

In summary, Anya believes that the problem lay in the religious abuse Natalia experienced and the ways this is impacting her ability to work through the domestic violence. Furthermore, the problem is complicated by Anya's lack of experience working with people who have experienced religious abuse and her own troubled relationship with religion.

## *Apply a Code of Ethics*

After identifying the problem, it is critical to consult with one's respective professional ethical codes. Forester-Miller and Davis (2016) recommend the *2014 ACA Code of Ethics*; however, as stated in Chapter 7, helping professionals may consult with their own respective codes. Because Anya is a licensed clinical mental health counselor, she consults the *2014 ACA Code of Ethics*.

Anya is first drawn to the code regarding respect and values imposition:

> Counselors are aware of—and avoid imposing—their own values, attitudes, beliefs, and behaviors. Counselors respect the diversity of clients, trainees, and research participants and seek training in areas in which they are at risk of imposing their values onto clients, especially when the counselor's values are inconsistent with the client's goals or are discriminatory in nature.
>
> (ACA, 2014, A.4.b)

Because of her troubled relationships with religion, Anya knows that she might unduly impose her values onto Natalia. Because of this, she considers the idea of consulting with a colleague or engaging in professional supervision.

Anya is also drawn to the ethical code on nondiscrimination:

> Counselors do not condone or engage in discrimination against prospective or current clients, students, employees, supervisees, or research participants based on age, culture, disability, ethnicity, race, religion/spirituality, gender, gender identity, sexual orientation, marital/ partnership status, language preference, socioeconomic status, immigration status, or any basis proscribed by law.
>
> (ACA, 2014, C.5)

Although Anya does not intend to discriminate against Natalia, she is aware of her impulse to refer Natalia to a professional who is more experienced at working with clients with religious issues. She is concerned about professional abandonment, but she is also aware of the following ethical code on boundaries of competence:

> Counselors practice only within the boundaries of their competence, based on their education, training, supervised experience, state and national professional credentials, and appropriate professional experience. Whereas multicultural counseling competency is required across all counseling specialties, counselors gain knowledge, personal awareness, sensitivity, dispositions, and skills pertinent to being a culturally competent counselor in working with a diverse client population.
>
> (ACA, 2014, C.2.a)

Based on these two ethical codes, Anya wonders if perhaps she needs more training in the area of religious abuse... and maybe even more training in the area of religion in general!

Finally, Anya is drawn to the ethical code about clients' support networks:

> Counselors recognize that support networks hold various meanings in the lives of clients and consider enlisting the support, understanding, and involvement of others (e.g., religious/ spiritual/community leaders, family members, friends) as positive resources, when appropriate, with client consent.
>
> (ACA, 2014, A.1.d)

Anya knows how important the church and church members are to Natalia, and although she is angry with Pastor Josiah, she also does not want to sever Natalia's relationship to her community. She wonders if she needs to consult with religious figures about this.

After reviewing the respective code of ethics, Anya begins to consider the following ideas: (1) consulting with a colleague to explore her own feelings around religion so they do not impact her work with Natalia, (2) attending a training in religious abuse, and (3) consulting with a religious figure in the community to gain more perspective on the issue. However, she continues to proceed through Forester-Miller and Davis's (2016) ethical decision-making model in order to gain a full picture of the issue.

### *Determine the Nature and Dimensions of the Dilemma*

According to Forester-Miller and Davis (2016), the problem should be further explored from multiple angles, more specifically (1) Kitchener's (1984) ethical principles, (2) scholarly literature, (3) experienced professionals, and (4) national and/or state associations. First, Anya considers Kitchener's (1984) ethical principles of autonomy, beneficence, nonmaleficence, fidelity, and justice. Anya recognizes the importance of Natalia's autonomy in her marriage and in her religious affiliation, and she does not want to undermine this. She also seeks to "do good" (beneficence) by honoring her beliefs and helping her work through the trauma of Pastor Josiah's words. Similarly, she wants to avoid doing any harm (nonmaleficence) by imposing some of her own values, experiences, and beliefs about religion. She also believes that referring Natalia would be harmful, as she and Natalia have established a trusting relationship. Additionally, Anya realizes the urgency of the domestic abuse and wants to, first and foremost, continue to ensure Natalia's safety. Finally, to guarantee justice and fidelity, Anya seeks to maintain a relationship with Natalia and serve her to the best of her ability, as she would her other clients.

After considering Kitchener's (1984) ethical principles, Anya explores scholarly literature related to religious abuse. She discovers Swindle and Cashwell's (2018) research on the three different types of religious abuse (abuse by a religious leader, abuse by a religious community, and abuse with a religious element) and determines that Natalia has experienced both abuse by a religious leader and abuse with a religious element. She continues to explore the professional literature on religious abuse, and this further confirms her decision that she needs more training in the area.

In addition to the scholarly literature, Anya briefly consults with a colleague (Jamison) in her practice. She describes the issue and asks for guidance on areas that she might be overlooking. Jamison agrees with her that she needs more training and needs to consult with a religious figure in the community for greater perspective and understanding.

Finally, Anya explores the state and national professional associations to see if they might provide her with more insight and guidance. Although she does not discover much guidance beyond the ethical codes, it is through the website that she learns of a training in treating spiritual abuse offered within the next month. Anya considers registering for it.

### *Generate Potential Courses of Action*

From here, Anya is in a position to develop some potential courses of action, which entails brainstorming ideas. Forester-Miller and Davis (2016)

## Application of Ethics in Treating Religious Abuse 71

encourage professionals to generate as many ideas as possible. Based on the previous steps, Anya generates the following list:

1. Register for the upcoming training (or any other training) focused on religious abuse.
2. Buy informational books on treating religious abuse in clients.
3. Read a memoir about a person's experience with religious abuse.
4. Attend a religious service to become more acquainted with the culture.
5. Watch documentaries about religious abuse.
6. Consult with a former colleague who has more experience treating people who have experienced religious abuse.
7. Meet with a religious leader in the community.
8. Read more about the specific nondenominational church with which Natalia belongs.
9. Engage in journaling to reflect upon her own experiences with religion.
10. Engage in personal counseling to explore her conflicting feelings about religion.
11. Find a supervisor (with experience in religious abuse) who can supervise her work with Natalia.
12. Join the Association for Spiritual, Ethical, and Religious Values in Counseling, and review their resources.
13. Read the Bible passages Natalia quoted and examine them from multiple theological perspectives.

### *Consider the Potential Consequences of All Options and Determine a Course of Action*

At this point, Anya is in a position to step back, review all of the options, and develop a course of action. Although she is partial to many of the ideas and believes that many – if not all – of them would help her with the problem, she also realizes that she does not have unlimited amounts of time and needs to be efficient, yet thorough, in her actions. Examining all of the options, she realizes that there are themes to her options: (1) increased education (through training, books, documentaries, articles, religious information, etc.), (2) personal exploration (through journaling, consulting with others, engaging in supervision), and (3) religious understanding (through religious figures, religious denominations, religious associations, etc.). Based on these themes, she decides on the following three courses of action:

1. Register for the training on treating religious abuse in clients.
2. Consult with a trusted colleague about her own conflicted feelings of religion.
3. Meet with a religious figure in the community to learn more about nondenominational churches and healing religious practices.

### Evaluate the Selected Course of Action

Drawing upon Stadler's (1986) work, Forester- Miller and Davis (2016) recommend helping professionals further evaluate their courses of action by answering three questions related to justice, publicity, and universality. The question related to justice is: Am I treating this client fairly? For publicity, it is: How would I feel if my actions were made public? And finally, universality incorporates the question: Would I recommend this same course of action to someone else?

Anya considers these questions very carefully, as she wants to ensure that she is providing the best care to Natalia. First, she questions whether or not she is treating the client fairly. Being aware of her own biases around religion, she recognizes the potential that she might *not* treat the client fairly and cause undue influence on her. However, because she has a plan for consulting with a colleague and processing her own feelings around religion, she feels as though she is working in a fair and just manner. In terms of publicity, Anya believes that her plan of action is sound and would be commended in public settings. She believes she is earnestly working toward increased education about religious abuse, monitoring her own biases, and seeking more understanding of religion in general. She feels as though this plan of action follows guidelines of best practice. Finally, Anya asks herself if she would recommend the same course of action to another colleague. She hesitates a bit on this one, wondering if she might encourage her colleague to refer the client to a counselor with more experience (and less bias). However, she also needs to take into account the repercussions of professional abandonment, which she believes would be especially damaging for Natalia. Therefore, she decides that, yes, this is the course of action that she would recommend.

### Implement the Course of Action

Anya first meets with a religious leader in the community, Pastor Amelia, and asks about Ephesians 5:22 and her thoughts on women submitting to their husbands in the name of God. She acknowledges the importance of the verse and further expounds upon the scripture by adding historical context and the responsibilities of men to their wives as described in Ephesians 5:28 (men should love their wives as their own bodies). Without knowing anything about the situation with Natalia (preserving full confidentiality), Pastor Amelia says that oftentimes Ephesians 5:22 is taken out of context – especially in cases of domestic abuse. She emphasizes the importance of knowing the totality of the biblical passages and the underlying love and devotion required of both partners. Anya believes this information might be really helpful to Natalia, so she asks Pastor Amelia if she would be okay with her providing her name as a referral source. Pastor Amelia readily agrees.

After her talk with Pastor Amelia, Anya finds that her own feelings about religion have softened some. However, as planned, she consults with her trusted colleague about her own biases. In their heartfelt discussion, Anya describes her past experiences with religion and the anger, disappointment, and sadness that she felt when she left the church. She says that she feels a sense of emptiness around religion now, and she sometimes suffers from existential anxiety. Furthermore, she is concerned about how all of these personal issues will impact her work with her client (keeping Natalia's story confidential). Her colleague listens patiently, offering validation and support throughout Anya's narrative. She says that from her vantage point, Anya is doing everything possible to examine her own biases and work ethically with her client. She does, however, follow this up with a recommendation to seek personal counseling, stating that Anya seems to be quite troubled by the religious confusion she feels in her own life. Anya agrees, deciding to continue her exploration of religion in personal counseling.

Finally, Anya registers for a training specifically focused on treating spiritual and religious abuse in clients. She learns about the types of abuse, the ways they manifest in clients, and various treatments that could be beneficial. Surprisingly, she also learns more about the ways that religious and spiritual interventions – when used appropriately – could be beneficial for clients.

With newfound knowledge and insight, Anya continues to work with Natalia. She refers her to Pastor Amelia, with whom Natalia develops a very close, lasting relationship. Furthermore, Anya helps Natalia begin to explore some of the ways her religious beliefs can give her strength in her decision to leave Chad for the time being and live with a friend. Natalia begins engaging in centering prayer, meditating on the biblical passage from Proverbs 31:25: "She is clothed with strength and dignity, and she laughs without fear of the future." Natalia continues to attend her beloved church; however, she consults with Pastor Amelia when faced with spiritual questions, rather than Pastor Josiah. With her newfound sense of strength, Natalia draws a boundary with Chad, informing him that if he ever wants to repair their relationship, he must seek his own help and stop drinking alcohol. Watching Natalia grow and deepen her relationship with God through this adversity inspires Anya to continue engaging in her own personal exploration of religion and spirituality. She soon finds connections in a local Quaker group and begins meditating daily.

Certainly, cases of religious and spiritual abuse are complex, and not all of them end as fortunately as Natalia's situation. However, guided by ethical principles, virtue ethics, a comprehensive decision-making model like Forester-Miller and Davis's (2016) model, and knowledge about (and training in treating) religious abuse, helping professionals can begin to help clients heal these sacred wounds.

## References

Cashwell, C., & Swindle, P. (2018). When religion hurts: Supervising cases of religious abuse. *The Clinical Supervisor, 37,* 182–203.

Forester-Miller, H., & Davis, T. E. (2016). *Practitioner's guide to ethical decision making* (Rev. ed.). Retrieved from http://www.counseling.org/docs/default-source/ethics/practioner's-guide-toethical-decision-making.pdf

Forester-Miller, H., & Rubenstein, R. L. (1992). Group counseling: Ethics and professional issues. In D. Capuzzi & D. R. Gross (Eds.), *Introduction to group counseling* (2nd ed., pp. 307–323). Denver, CO: Love.

Haas, L. J., & Malouf, J. L. (1989). *Keeping up the good work: A practitioner's guide to mental health ethics.* Sarasota, FL: Professional Resource Exchange.

Kitchener, K. S. (1984). Intuition, critical evaluation and ethical principles: The foundation for ethical decisions in counseling psychology. *Counseling Psychologist, 12,* 43–55.

Stadler, H. A. (1986). Making hard choices: Clarifying controversial ethical issues. *Counseling and Human Development, 19,* 1–10.

Van Hoose, W. H., & Paradise, L. V. (1979). *Ethics in counseling and psychotherapy: Perspectives in issues and decision making.* Cranston, RI: Carroll.

# Section III
# Treatment Approaches

# 9 The Importance of a Trauma-Informed Approach

There are many different theoretical frameworks and techniques that a therapist might employ when working with someone with a history of religious abuse. Whichever theory or technique is used with the client, it will be helpful to consider the religious abuse in light of a trauma-informed lens.

The trauma that can occur in experiences of religious abuse can include emotional trauma such as Post Traumatic Stress Disorder (PTSD); betrayal trauma due to feeling betrayed by the church, religion, family, church leaders, or even God; and spiritual trauma such as conflating a religious leader with God. We go into more detail about the experience of betrayal in Chapter 3, but as a reminder betrayal trauma is a trauma in which "the people or institutions on which a person depends for survival significantly violates that person's trust or well-being" (Freyd, 2008, p. 76).

When therapists utilize trauma-informed care, they are aware of and address the possibility of effects on the individual in a wide variety of ways including biological, psychological, social, and neurological impacts. Trauma-informed counselors understand that people who are seeking mental health care have a high prevalence of trauma in their history, and therefore assess trauma in all clients. Trauma-informed therapists are not problematizing their clients and seeking to discover what is "wrong" with them, but rather seeking to understand their experience and "what happened to them." (CDC, 2020; SAMHSA, 2014)

It is vital that counselors treating clients with a history of religious abuse understand the importance of safety and acceptance in the counseling space, and that the client trusts the therapist can handle their pain and trauma around a sometimes heated topic such as religious beliefs and experiences. These are clients who have been harmed by someone or a system in which they may have placed their utmost trust and experienced betrayal from someone as important as a Higher Power. They may not trust their therapist very quickly.

Clients with a history of religious harm may not even label it as trauma and may need help understanding the severity of the impact on them (Cashwell & Swindle, 2018). The counselor also needs to be aware of possible triggers to the client such as religious language or symbols in a therapist office.

DOI: 10.4324/9781003029465-12

In order to build trust, such a client may ask more pointed questions about the therapist's religious beliefs. Although there is no one right answer when it comes to self-disclosure, it is important that the therapist share as much as they feel comfortable and are honest in whatever they choose to disclose, and that they convey unconditional positive regard and nonjudgment. Counselors should also be aware of their own reactions and any personal trauma that might be activated by these clients.

Some clients may be traumatized by their grief and loss that is connected to their religious abuse (Cashwell & Swindle, 2018). It can be traumatic to be rejected by one's family as a result of your identity or deconstructing beliefs. When faith is weaponized in such a conflict, the trauma may be amplified.

Trauma is often accompanied by feelings of loss of power and loss of control. As described in earlier chapters, the issue of power and control are often factors in the dynamics of religious abuse, with the sacred element being used as the ultimate power and control (Cashwell & Swindle, 2018). An important part of the therapeutic process often involves the client regaining a sense of power and control in relation to their religious systems and beliefs.

Specific interventions will be discussed in upcoming chapters but should only be used after the therapist gains a strong understanding of the ways in which a trauma-informed lens can be beneficial to the therapeutic process.

# References

Cashwell, C. S., & Swindle, P. S. (2018). When religion hurts: Supervising cases of religious abuse. *The Clinical Supervisor, 37*(1), 182–203. doi: 10.1080/07325223.2018.1443205

Centers for Disease Control (CDC). (2020). *Infographic: 6 guiding principles to a trauma-informed approach*. Retrieved May 21, 2023 from https://www.cdc.gov/orr/infographics/6_principles_trauma_info.htm.

Freyd, J. J. (2008). Betrayal trauma. In G. Reyes, J. D. Elhai & J. D. Ford (Eds.), *Encyclopedia of psychological trauma* (pp. 76). New York: Wiley.

Substance Abuse and Mental Health Services Administration. SAMHSA's Concept of Trauma and Guidance for a Trauma- Informed Approach. (2014). *HHS Publication No. (SMA) 14-4884*. Rockville, MD: Substance Abuse and Mental Health Services Administration. Retrieved from: https://ncsacw.samhsa.gov/userfiles/files/SAMHSA_Trauma.pdf

# 10 The Healing Process

This chapter will explore some of the ways victims of religious abuse have experienced healing, including exiting the religious system, finding new religious communities, staying in the religious system with other types of support, seeking counseling, and focusing energy on helping others. Specific interventions will be discussed in Chapter 10, but this chapter will focus on some overall experiences that have been helpful in the process of recovering from religious abuse.

Some clients will report that they were helped by exiting the system in which the abuse occurred (Swindle, 2017). Many do choose to discontinue involvement in their church or ministry group, and while there is often a grieving process, once they are out and the broken connection is clear, it is often a relief for clients. They no longer have to engage with their abuser(s). They are no longer reminded of their betrayal trauma from various sources including religious leaders, fellow congregants, or their own theology or belief systems. This can be a very freeing experience for the client, as they may have been raised in this system and never felt that they had an option about whether or not to attend and belong. Continuously or repeatedly being exposed to your abuse/trauma triggers is very hard on the nervous system, the emotional state, and the mental health of a person, so it may take some time to release, but once someone has broken ties with a religious system that abused them, there is often a very healing corrective experience (Cashwell & Swindle, 2018; Swindle, 2017).

However, therapists should understand that not everyone who has experienced religious abuse chooses to disconnect from the system in which it occurred. This can be confusing and seem irrational to some (including the therapist), but it is important to allow the client to own this decision and not to impose a course of action. There may be many reasons a client chooses to stay (family or friend connections, their own faith, convenience, connections of their children, enjoy some aspects and can separate from the abuse, etc.), and they may be coming to counseling with the goal of gaining coping skills to manage this choice. It is important that the client feel autonomous and empowered to make this decision (Cashwell & Swindle, 2018). Therapists

DOI: 10.4324/9781003029465-13

should also understand that this may be an evolving issue in the therapeutic process, and they may need support as they choose to leave or return to the system or work through potential ambivalence about this.

In addition, therapists should not make assumptions about what disconnecting (or not) from the religious organization implies about one's faith. Some may choose to leave this system and maintain their own personal beliefs without a religious structure in place. Some may leave, completely deconstruct, and release any religious belief. Some may leave, maintain or adapt their beliefs, and seek out a healthier religious system. Some may continue in their religious system and still deconstruct or abandon some or all of their faith. There are many scenarios here, but the main takeaway for therapists is that religious involvement and belief are not always tied, and the client may need therapeutic support for either the religious community issues, the potential existential crisis and/or deconstruction process, or both.

Connected to this is that some people describe their ability to separate their abuse from God or from their own beliefs to be helpful. Some may have the thought of "That wasn't God who hurt me, that was a human" and find this comforting. This can also decrease the levels of betrayal they feel.

Clients often describe healing coming from eventually feeling heard in their experiences of religious abuse and validation of those feelings/experiences, especially if they never got that from the system in which the abuse occurred. For example, someone who was shamed by their pastor for using psychotropic medication such as antidepressants may experience a great deal of validation if they move to a healthier religious system and hear someone in their Sunday school class mention their own antidepressants, or if the pastor encourages use of prescribed medication in a sermon. It is common for the abuse to occur, and for people to be retraumatized by the dismissal of the abuse on many levels, so having someone such as a friend or counselor validate that the experience was indeed abuse, and was indeed traumatic can be very helpful (Swindle, 2017).

Many do report that seeking counseling has been helpful for them (Swindle, 2017), which underscores the importance of counselors feeling equipped to assess and address religious harm in the counseling space.

## References

Cashwell, C. S., & Swindle, P. S. (2018). When religion hurts: Supervising cases of religious abuse. *The Clinical Supervisor, 37*(1), 182–203. doi: 10.1080/07325223.2018.1443305

Swindle, Paula J. (2017). *A twisting of the sacred: The lived experience of religious abuse*. The University of North Carolina at Greensboro, ProQuest Dissertations Publishing. 10264116.

# 11 Interventions for Religious Abuse

Because there are so many different types and experiences of religious abuse, the types of therapeutic intervention that are most appropriate to each client also vary greatly. However, there are some interventions that may be especially helpful for this population that therapists will want to consider, including

- Motivational Interviewing
- Internal Family Systems
- Trauma specific approaches (Eye Movement Desensitization and Reprocessing (EMDR), Somatic Experiencing, Sensorimotor Psychotherapy, Trauma-Focused Cognitive Behavioral Therapy (CBT), and Prolonged Exposure therapy.

## Motivational Interviewing

The components of Motivational Interviewing can provide a grounding for mental health professionals in all aspects of addressing issues of religion and spirituality with a client. This topic can create some unease in therapists, particularly around the concern not imposing the therapist's own beliefs or values on the client, and Motivational Interviewing's focus on client autonomy can help alleviate some of that concern (Giordano & Cashwell, 2014).

The topic of religious abuse can be a loaded and triggering one for clients and for counselors, and many people have strong reactions to this. It can already be difficult for therapists to remain objective on the topic of spirituality, and when you bring in the element of abuse in a religious setting, there are often emotional and sometimes challenging transference and countertransference at play. Counselors may be biased because they are religious and feel the need to defend God and the idea of church. Counselors may be biased because they are anti-religious and feel hostile toward it and wish to direct a client away from religion – or anywhere in between on that continuum. Because it is imperative that clients who have experienced religious abuse are given a counseling space free from judgment of any kind, the tenants of

DOI: 10.4324/9781003029465-14

Motivational Interviewing that focus on the client's motivation and autonomy can help create this safe therapeutic space for the client to process their own experience.

Motivational Interviewing may also be used at the rapport building stage, and then transition in a more trauma-focused approach.

*Internal Family Systems*

One of the more trauma-focused approaches that might be helpful when working with clients how have experienced religious abuse is an Internal Family Systems approach. In their book *Internal Family Systems Therapy*, Schwartz and Sweezy (2020) describe Internal Family Systems as "a synthesis of two paradigms: the plural mind, or the idea that we all contain many different parts, and systems thinking" (p. 4). Internal Family Systems allows the client to identify different "parts" of themselves and to give voice to all of those different parts in a nonjudgmental way.

This approach may be especially helpful for clients with a history of religious abuse because there are often so many aspects of one's identity at play. As discussed earlier, a client may have conflicting emotions and desires around leaving the religious organization in which they experienced harm. There may be a very loyal part of them that wants to remain a part of the system, and there may be a very protective part that wants to get them out of this system. Using an Internal Family Systems approach, the client can give voice to both of these parts without judgment and work through how they are both trying to help or serve her in some way.

Parts work can be very helpful for a client who is deconstructing their religious beliefs, often as a result of harm that occurred to them in their religious life. For example, a client who was raised in a strong purity culture may no longer believe that way, but does not understand why they still have "baggage" around their sex life. Clients who have deconstructed may feel shame for their earlier beliefs and want to bury that part of themselves, but Internal Family Systems work can help them accept the different stages of their life and how the parts might still show up from time to time in order to protect them in the best way they know how. This can help the client to release some of their self-described "baggage."

*Trauma-Informed Approaches*

As described in Chapter 9, most clients who have suffered religious abuse would benefit from a counselor working through a trauma-informed lens. Religious abuse may include several types of trauma including emotional trauma, betrayal trauma, and spiritual trauma. This trauma may be experienced on multiple levels including biological, mental, emotional, spiritual, and psychological. Therefore, any of the trauma-informed approaches such as EMDR,

Somatic Experiencing, Sensorimotor Psychotherapy, Trauma-Focused CBT, and Prolonged Exposure therapy may be aligned with the goals of the client. Therapists should work with their clients to find an approach that will meet the needs of the client best or refer to someone with trauma-informed expertise if the counselor does not have that.

# References

Giordano, A. L., & Cashwell, C. S. (2014). Entering the sacred: Using motivational interviewing to address spirituality in counseling. *Counseling and Values, 59,* 65–79.

Schwartz & Sweezy. (2020). *Internal family systems therapy.* New York: Guilford Press.

# 12 Supervision and Consultation

This chapter describes the importance of engaging in clinical supervision and consultation when working with cases of religious abuse. Additionally, it will provide guidance for supervisors and how to help supervisees manage their own emotional reactivity and personal bias when working with cases of religious abuse. Additionally, this chapter provides information on ways therapists can provide consultation services to religious systems to prevent or decrease the potential for religious abuse.

Supervisors can be a critical piece to ensuring appropriate assessment of religious abuse. They should be broaching aspects of culture and identity with their supervisees, both to process how they might impact the supervisory relationship and to ensure the client is broaching those topics with their clients.

As described in earlier chapters, working with the subject of religious abuse can be a very intense and reactive experience. It is normal for the therapist to experience a wide range of emotions and triggers themselves while working with such a client. Because there is so much potential for emotion reactivity and room for the imposition of values all along the continuum of religious counselors to anti-religious counselors, we highly recommend therapists who work with religious abuse clients seek regular consultation or supervision, and that newer, provisional licensed therapists bring client with a religious abuse history to their regular supervision sessions (Cashwell & Swindle, 2018).

For these reasons, it is imperative that clinical supervisors provide a safe and nonjudgmental supervision space for counselors to be honest about ways they might be struggling, their own reactions, or their fear of imposition (Cashwell & Swindle, 2018). Supervisors should bear in mind the five components of effective trauma-informed supervision suggested by Berger and Quiros (2014) (i.e., safety, trustworthiness, choice, collaboration, and empowerment). This kind of supervisory relationship and rapport can help the supervisor to assess a more accurate development of skills of the supervisee and whether or not they are equipped to handle the multiple types of trauma that may emerge in counseling victims of religious abuse.

The supervision space should be a parallel process of the counseling process. While the counselor strives to maintain client autonomy, the supervisor also strives to maintain counselor autonomy. In a similar fashion, the supervisor should be continually checking in with themselves to address any bias they may feel on the topic of religious abuse and can model this self-reflection and vulnerability for their supervisees (Cashwell & Swindle, 2018).

As supervisors become more confident in their ability to supervise cases of religious abuse, they may consider ways they could provide consultation in other areas. In Chapter 5, we discussed the characteristics of healthy religious systems versus unhealthy religious systems. Supervisors might want to consider offering consultation services to religious systems, either as an assessment process for the health of their system and how vulnerable they are to occurrences of religious abuse or providing support and guidance when a church or other religious organization experiences religious abuse.

In those cases where the system has exposed an incident(s) of religious abuse, there will be individuals who need counseling, and there will also be needs in the system to investigate, support the accuser(s), and create a plan for restorative justice or accountability. There will be opportunities in these instances for the system to grow and heal, but they will need guidance and support, and counselors who have an understanding of religious abuse will be great consultation resources for something like this.

## References

Berger, R., & Quiros, L. (2014). Supervision for trauma-informed practice. *Traumatology, 20,* 296–301. doi: 10.1037/h0099835

Cashwell, C. S., & Swindle, P. S. (2018). When religion hurts: Supervising cases of religious abuse. *The Clinical Supervisor, 37*(1), 182–203. doi: 10.1080/07325223.2018.1443305

# 13 Summary

The phenomenon of religious abuse, sometimes called "spiritual abuse, religious trauma, or religious harm", is not new, but understanding how to treat it is new to the mental health field. As part of a thorough assessment, therapists should be assessing for the spiritual/religious worldview (or lack thereof) of their clients. Counselors have some general understanding of how positive and supportive experiences may be used in the counseling process at the client's request as part of their coping, meaning-making, or support systems. However, mental health professionals are severely lacking in guidance for how to work with clients who may present with negative religious experiences, including that which may be considered religious abuse. It is our hope that this book has provided some guidance in this area.

Therapists should not only broach the subject of religious or spiritual identity but go deeper into the topic, explicitly inviting their clients to share their religious or spiritual experiences and creating a safe counseling space for clients to share experiences of religious harm. There are not a lot of formal assessments on the topic outside of Koch and Edstrom's (2022) Religious Harm and Abuse Scale, but therapists should do more qualitative in-depth assessments of religious harm during the intake process and throughout the counseling process as needed. Religious abuse may also present as a part of other trauma or mental health diagnoses such as PTSD, substance use, or depression, so more general assessments may be appropriate.

Experiences of religious abuse typically fall into one or more of three broad categories:

1 Abuse perpetrated by religious leadership, typically an individual leader
2 Abuse perpetrated by a religious group, directed either toward an individual or toward a group of people
3 Abuse in which the abuse itself has a religious component to it (Swindle, 2017).

These three categories capture the wide range and variety of experiences that may fall under the umbrella of religious abuse. Religious abuse can include any emotional, physical, or sexual abuse committed that has a connection to a religion or a religious organization (Cashwell & Swindle, 2018). Common experiences that occur with this type of abuse include trauma, feelings of betrayal, feelings of powerless and lack of control, confusion about their faith, isolation, and grief responses.

Occurrences of religious abuse can happen in any religious system, but systems that have a very rigid and hierarchical leadership structure that lacks transparency and concentrates power at the top may be more likely to have incidents of religious abuse. These are often systems that do not allow questions of authority including the leadership and the theology they are espousing, and often claim their leadership is ordained by God and makes them closer to God and therefore should not be questioned (Swindle, 2017).

On the other hand, healthier religious systems include a high level of transparency and openness at every level including leadership, a shared governance, and a valuing of people and relationships over that of power and rules. Religious abuse could happen to anyone, but there are some populations who are particularly vulnerable to religious abuse, including women, members of the LGBTQ+ (Lesbian, Gay, Bisexual, Transgender, Queer+) community, children, racial/ethnic minorities, pastors, those who have left religious systems and are deconstructing, and those who not share the religion of the dominant culture.

Because of the high levels of emotion and potential reactivity around the topic of religious abuse, it is critical that therapists engage in self-examination around the ethics of not imposing and client autonomy. There is potential for bias all along the continuum of highly religious counselors who feel defensive of religion and those, on the other end, who are hostile toward religion and see now value. Supervision and consultation is an essential part of this self-examination, and supervisors should be prepared to do their own work while supporting and guiding supervisees in the assessment for religious abuse and encouraging reflective practice.

Many types of trauma may be experienced in religious abuse, including emotional trauma, betrayal trauma, and spiritual trauma. Therefore, therapists working with religious abuse clients should consider their work through a trauma-informed lens. Several trauma-informed approaches can be utilized with this topic including Internal Family Systems, trauma-specific approaches such as Eye Movement Desensitization and Reprocessing (EMDR), Somatic Experiencing, Sensorimotor Psychotherapy, Trauma-Focused Cognitive Behavioral Therapy (CBT), and Prolonged Exposure therapy. Aspects of Motivational Interviewing can also be useful to ensure client autonomy.

Healing from religious abuse can take many forms, but client autonomy is key to all of them. Clients may have several different reactions and outcomes – some may stay in the system in which they experienced abuse, and some may choose to leave. Some may deconstruct their own religious beliefs; some may not. Some may separate their experiences from their faith; some may conflate them and feel abused and betrayed by both a human(s) and the system and larger theology. Some clients who seek counseling have reported finding it helpful (Swindle, 2017).

Experiences of religious abuse can be very damaging to clients, but there are many ways therapists can provide assistance to these clients to help them recover. As our understanding of the phenomena of religious abuse continues to grow, it is hoped that therapists like you will commit to assisting your individual clients, as well as advocating for changes in larger systems to help them be more healthy.

## References

Cashwell, C. S., & Swindle, P. S. (2018). When religion hurts: Supervising cases of religious abuse. *The Clinical Supervisor, 37*(1), 182–203. doi: 10.1080/07325223.2018. 1443305

Koch, D., & Edstrom, L. (2022). Development of the spiritual harm and abuse scale. *Journal for the Scientific Study of Religion, 61*, 476–506. doi: 10.1111/jssr.12792

Swindle, Paula J. (2017). *A twisting of the sacred: The lived experience of religious abuse*. The University of North Carolina at Greensboro, ProQuest Dissertations Publishing. 10264116.

# Index

ACA code of ethics 38, 54, 58, 68–69
ASERVIC 25, 27, 38–39
assessment 20, 25, 38–40, 84–88

betrayal 5, 32–36, 40, 51, 77, 79–80, 82, 87; betrayal trauma 5, 77, 79, 82

categories of religious abuse 26, 29–30, 33, 39, 44, 86
control 12, 14–15, 17, 35–36, 41–42, 46, 55, 64, 78, 87

deconstruction 34, 44, 46–47, 78, 80, 82, 87

EMDR 81–82, 87
existential 17, 32–34, 46, 73, 80

grief 32–36, 47, 78, 87

IFS *see* Internal Family Systems
Internal Family Systems 81–83, 87

interventions 58, 61–62, 73, 78, 79, 81–83; *see also* techniques

LGBTQ+ 7, 28, 33, 36, 42, 44–46, 87

manipulation 32, 35
motivational interviewing 13, 22, 23, 81–83

pastors 6, 44, 47, 87
powerlessness 32, 35–36, 52, 87

religious coping 12–14, 22
religious leader 3, 14, 16–18, 26–29, 32–34, 39, 41–46, 54, 59–61, 69–72, 77, 79, 86–87
rules 32, 35–36, 43, 46, 52, 87

supervision 57–58, 68, 71, 84–85, 87

techniques 58, 77; *see also* interventions
theory 77
trauma-informed 36, 57, 60–63